ARCHITECTURE IS LIFE

ARCHITECTURE IS LIFE

Edited by Mohsen Mostafavi

Lars Müller Publishers

6 **PREFACE**
Farrokh Derakhshani

9 **THE ARCHITECTURE OF LIFE**
Mohsen Mostafavi

26 **STEERING COMMITTEE BRIEF**

29 **REPORT OF THE MASTER JURY**

34 **THE PARTICULAR AND THE UNIVERSAL**
Mahmood Mamdani

42 **GEOGRAPHY AND ARCHITECTURE**
David Adjaye

46 **INNOVATION AND JUDGEMENT**
Toshiko Mori

50 **THE AWARD AND CHINA**
Wang Shu

51 **ENDLESS INVENTIVENESS**
Shahzia Sikander

CRAFT

54 **PRESERVATION OF THE MBARU NIANG**
Wae Rebo Village, Flores Island, Indonesia

64 **KANTANA FILM AND ANIMATION INSTITUTE**
Nakhon Pathom, Thailand

74 **MAPUNGUBWE INTERPRETATION CENTRE**
Limpopo Province, South Africa

83 **BUILDING CRAFTS IN THE MODERN WORLD**
Omar Abdulaziz Hallaj

CONSERVATION

90 **PRESERVATION OF SACRED AND COLLECTIVE OASIS SITES**
Guelmim Region, Morocco

100 **RESTORATION OF THULA FORT**
Yemen

110 **REVITALISATION OF BIRZEIT HISTORIC CENTRE** 2013 AWARD RECIPIENT
Palestine

126 **REHABILITATION OF NAGAUR FORT**
Rajasthan, India

DWELLING

138 **APARTMENT NO. 1**
Mahallat, Iran

148 **THE MET TOWER**
Bangkok, Thailand

INFRASTRUCTURE

- 162 **REHABILITATION OF TABRIZ BAZAAR** 2013 AWARD RECIPIENT
  Iran
- 180 **RABAT-SALÉ URBAN INFRASTRUCTURE PROJECT** 2013 AWARD RECIPIENT
  Morocco
- 198 **ISLAMIC CEMETERY** 2013 AWARD RECIPIENT
  Altach, Austria
- 216 **SALAM CENTRE FOR CARDIAC SURGERY** 2013 AWARD RECIPIENT
  Khartoum, Sudan

- 233 **PLACENESS AND WELL-BEING, THROUGH THE LENS OF INFRASTRUCTURE**
  Hanif Kara

INSTITUTION

- 240 **LYCÉE FRANÇAIS CHARLES DE GAULLE**
  Damascus, Syria
- 250 **MOHAMMED VI FOOTBALL ACADEMY**
  Salé, Morocco
- 260 **MUSEUM OF HANDCRAFT PAPER**
  Gaoligong, Yunnan, China

RESILIENCE

- 272 **UMUBANO PRIMARY SCHOOL**
  Kigali, Rwanda
- 282 **POST-TSUNAMI HOUSING**
  Kirinda, Sri Lanka
- 292 **MARIA GRAZIA CUTULI PRIMARY SCHOOL**
  Khushrud Village, Herat, Afghanistan
- 302 **RECONSTRUCTION OF NAHR EL-BARED REFUGEE CAMP**
  Akkar, Lebanon

- 316 **ON LANDSCAPE**
  Michel Desvigne

- 320 **TURKISH ARCHITECTURE TODAY!**
  Hashim Sarkis in conversation with Han Tümertekin and Murat Tabanlıoğlu

- 331 **REDEFINING THE BUILT PROJECT**
  Mohammad al-Asad

- 339 **FROM PUBLIC SPACE TO PUBLIC SPHERE**
  Homi K. Bhabha

- 346 2013 Award Steering Committee
  2013 Award Master Jury
- 347 2013 Award On-Site Reviewers
- 348 Award Recipients 1980–2013
- 350 Acknowledgements

PREFACE
Farrokh Derakhshani

Some four decades ago, rapid change and transformation in built environments had reached crisis levels in a great number of countries. New models of building were being adopted or imposed and were not responsive to the needs of communities faced with the deterioration and loss of existing traditions; the conflict between global trends and local requirements had become apparent both in architecture and in the societies for whom such architecture was intended. Observing this led His Highness the Aga Khan to establish the Award for Architecture in 1977, with the hope and objective of creating a platform to search for common experiences and examples that would point to directions for the enhancement of the built environment for future generations. From the very beginning, it was vital to conceive and nurture a dynamic process that would keep the Award at the vanguard of contemporary thought and ensure its present and future relevance. The Award embodies the belief that culture in general – and that architecture, the tangible manifestation of culture, in particular – is an essential vector of social development and cohesion.

It is in this manner and spirit that the Aga Khan Award for Architecture strives to stimulate discourse on the betterment of human life through the built environment. This monograph features the dialogues initiated and the path taken by the Award during the three-year period from 2011 to 2013, the 12th triennial cycle since the Award was founded. The directions taken by the Steering Committee reflect the specificity of this particular cycle – yet it is also aware of the Award's continued existence over time and the need to integrate the issues and debates of each cycle into a vision for the future. The process began with the hundreds of nominators around the world who contribute by identifying recently completed projects that are already in use. The Steering Committee identified an initial set of pertinent challenges and issues confronting contemporary societies that are reflected in the built environments; and it is the Steering Committee that selected the members of the independent 2013 Master Jury who, in their turn, debated these challenges and issues, as well as others brought forward by them, in the context of the actual building projects submitted and documented for the triennial Award. During this cycle, the Master Jury studied the pool of 411 nominated projects and selected amongst them a shortlist of 20 finalist projects, each exceptional in its own right. Experts conducted thorough On-Site Reviews of the shortlisted projects, after which the Master Jury selected five of them to be the recipients of the 2013 Awards.

In his introduction, Steering Committee member Mohsen Mostafavi describes the dynamics of the Award process, and the rigour and constancy of dialogue and debate that characterise it. In his essay "The Particular and the Universal", Mahmood Mamdani, Chair of the Master Jury, addresses some of the complex free-ranging topics and multifaceted issues that informed the Jury in its deliberations, and other members of the Jury have written on further topics for discussion and consideration. The volume concludes with an afterword by Steering Committee member Homi Bhabha, addressing the concept of the quality of life within the context of the Aga Khan Award, and other Committee members have contributed essays on ideas essential to the ongoing evolution of the Award. Throughout, we believe that the projects presented in this volume demonstrate unique and creative solutions for the communities in which they are built, and contain lessons for professionals all around the world. These past three years reflect yet another step in the Award's journey in search of architecture to enhance the quality of life for future generations of human society.

THE ARCHITECTURE OF LIFE
Mohsen Mostafavi

The Aga Khan Award for Architecture is based on a premise – a belief that architecture has the capacity to transform life. The pursuit of this conviction in many ways makes the Award unique within the growing landscape of architectural awards and prizes.

Throughout the history of the Award there has been an emphasis on socially transformative projects. This cycle of the Award is no exception. Premiated as well as shortlisted projects provide the framework for a host of activities. How these projects function is enhanced by the quality, the design and the materials of architecture.

The duality between architecture and life is not limited to the programme or the intentions of a project. Rather, it is the specific manner in which a project's aspirations are conceived and constructed that provides the critical basis for evaluation and judgment. This approach seeks innovative solutions that transcend local norms and practices. In doing so, the Award recognises past achievements while promoting and articulating the circumstances for best practice for the future.

One of the unique features of the Award is the tripartite relationship between the Steering Committee of the Award with the Master Jury and the On-Site Reviewers. Each group has its own domain of responsibilities with certain overlaps between the Steering Committee and the Master Jury, and between the Master Jury and the On-Site Reviewers. The Steering Committee works closely with His Highness the Aga Khan and the directorate of the Award to establish the broader context, including the themes, for each cycle of the Award. They select the Master Jury and address the impact of the Award's series of events, seminars, lectures, films and publications through each cycle.

The discussions between the Steering Committee and the Master Jury safeguard the thematic continuity and concerns of the Award.

For example, recently there has been a concerted effort to consider the role and importance of alternative and productive methods of planning and to debate and document both the history as well as the emergent conditions of spaces of work. This evolved from discussions of the Steering Committee and subsequently led to a conference in Istanbul; the outcome of which has been produced as a book on the subject. The primary purpose of these efforts is to advance our knowledge of specific sectors of the design field and in the process to reveal the necessity for greater stress on a chosen topic of significance. In this case, it was the question concerning current and future models of spaces of work, such as offices, workshops and factories.

The latest cycle of the Award builds on its history of innovative typological and thematic categories pertaining to the built environment. These groupings are invariably contingent on the diversity and range of projects submitted by the participants in a particular cycle of the Award. The Master Jury then shortlists a number of projects that they consider worthy of further investigation. These projects are visited and subjected to careful evaluation by a member of the On-Site Review group. The methodical on-site investigation of each project, its programme, design and execution, forms an important component of the Master Jury's decision-making process.

Equally important is the post-occupancy evaluation of each project – its conditions of construction and use. The utility of each project forms a partial description of its life as a building, landscape or artefact. Hence the premiated projects are those that in the opinion of the Master Jury – through debate, disagreement and dialogue – best articulate the multiple criteria of design excellence and responsive and innovative use of materials and construction.

Another component of the decision-making process is the broader physical impact of the project. The on-site visits by the reviewers also provide indispensable evidence of how a project is used by and benefits its constituency of users. The combinatory effect of this process, the establishment of an overall intellectual context by the Steering Committee, the deliberations of the Master Jury informed by the first-hand expert evidence of the On-Site Reviewers, are all part of a process that is intended to protect the integrity of the Award. One of the intentional consequences of this process is the attention given to modest as well as more complex design projects. Specifically, it is the visits by the On-Site Reviewers that furnish the Master Jury with the appropriate information to make decisions that are not simply based on photographic documentation of the submitted projects.

During the last cycle of the Award in 2010, the shortlisted projects were presented under five separate categories. These included environment, institution, industry, dwelling and conservation. In the current cycle, based on the decisions of the Master Jury, the categories have evolved into such topics as infrastructure, conservation, dwelling, craft and resilience – introducing changes while allowing for continuities. It is important to mention that none of these thematic clusters are purely exclusive. Rather, there is a certain fluidity between them. The intent is to highlight the value of the specific theme and to point out ways in which other projects might benefit from the knowledge gained.

Perhaps due to the lack of large-scale environmental projects like the Wadi Hanifa Wetlands in Riyadh, Saudi Arabia, in the last cycle, there has been more emphasis on the topic of infrastructure during the 2013 cycle of the Award. But in this case, infrastructure is not just limited to the description of a technical artefact. The Master Jury has been specific in designating a wider role for the topic of infrastructure, at times incorporating larger environmental concerns. The category in this book includes the Rabat-Salé Urban Infrastructure Project in Morocco, a piece of social infrastructure that connects two communities, as well as a hospital in Sudan. The term infrastructure, therefore, is seen as an enabling mechanism. It is an active or pro-active device.

In the case of the hospital, a cardiac surgery unit near Khartoum, Sudan, the 95 shipping containers that were used to send material to the site were deployed as one of its building blocks. These elements, together with a double insulation system, form part of the project's multiple sustainability strategies. In fact, the focus on sustainability is one of the principal elements that helps shape many of the shortlisted and premiated projects. Another example is the use of wind-assisted chimneys and retractable awnings in the Lycée Français Charles de Gaulle building in Damascus, Syria.

A different example of the concept of infrastructure is the Islamic Cemetery in Altach, Austria. The conferral of an Award represents the first recognition of a project that responds to needs of the diaspora community of Muslims in Europe. Austria, like many other European countries, is now experiencing the impact of second-generation immigrants who, having been born there, also wish to be buried in the country. This project, envisaged as one for a specific community, relies on the simplicity of its form and the permanence of its basic material – coloured concrete – to achieve the necessary monumentality and solemnity befitting its subject.

The 2013 cycle of the Aga Khan Award for Architecture also includes a larger than normal share of conservation projects. This of course varies from one cycle to the other, but it also demonstrates a positive trend in the appreciation of living heritage – of making the past a part of the present. In the case of some of the projects, for example the work carried out in the city of Birzeit, there is an overlap between conservation, infrastructure and craft. Those involved in this project have been particularly clear about seeing the conservation of the historic, former university town not as an end in itself but as the provision of an infrastructure for the revitalisation of the town and of its intangible heritage. The process of implementation of the project also necessitated the reliance on traditional crafts and a deeper understanding of the way things are made. Ultimately the project is a manifestation of the political will of the citizens to transform their community.

There is a parallel situation between this project and another recipient of the Award, the Bazaar in the city of Tabriz, Iran. The conservation of this historically significant urban artefact that had fallen into a state of disrepair is seen as a significant component of bringing life and commerce back to the Bazaar. The condition and quality of the architecture of this urban infrastructure is a crucial component of its role as a magnet for the public.

The specific attention given to craft, or rather the craft of making things, is not a mere consequence of dealing with conservation projects. In many parts of the Muslim world, the tools and techniques of construction have not kept pace with developments in other parts of the world. This has positive as well as negative consequences. The complexities and lack of industrialised building processes in many areas place more emphasis on small- and medium-scale operations for building construction. In some cases, conservation projects help keep certain techniques or crafts related to building construction alive. In many cases, the existing building acts as a palimpsest – a manual for how things were made in the past – and as a device for learning. The importance of this process should not be underestimated. The recovery of certain traditions provides the basis for new forms of knowledge that can be modified and used in other contexts in the future.

The contemporary apartment and retail building in the ancient town of Mahallat, Iran, is a modern edifice, one that would not be out of place in a European city. However, the use of recycled stone from a nearby quarry has resulted in the design of a building that combines contemporary design with an understanding of local materials. The architect used different colour stones of the same thickness to create a variegated stone facade. The contemporaneity of the project was balanced in the context of a conservative community through the use of local materials and the narrative of using "worthless" recycled stone. The construction and crafting of this building is at once modern and rooted. It is particular in ways that remind one of the site-specific Stone Walls of the British artist Andy Goldsworthy.

This cycle also sees an emphasis on the crucial topics of risk and resilience. This category can potentially include projects that deal with climate change to those that deal with the after-effects of earthquakes and tsunamis. It can also address the impact of human devastation, as is the case with the Nahr el-Bared Refugee Camp in Akkar, Lebanon. In this and other projects, the lines between risk mitigation, rebuilding and activism become blurred. In the case of the Camp, it would probably have been easier for the architects to build new shelters for the inhabitants. But, in their view, that would have returned the inhabitants to the status of living on a campsite. Instead, they opted for rebuilding on the ruins of the old camp and, in the process, incorporating its many layers of history and public spaces. Similarly, the refusal to build an emergency shelter is also evident in the Post-Tsunami Housing in Kirinda, Sri Lanka. Here the team emphasised their commitment to the community by designing and building houses that respond to the cultural needs of the users as well as to the climate and local materials. This approach departs from seeing architecture as neutral, devoid of local specificities and contingencies.

Each of the projects shortlisted or premiated by the 2013 Aga Khan Award for Architecture exhibits ideas that make a contribution to our understanding of what design can do. Each, in turn, also provides the framework – the infrastructure – for human activity. It is in the manner in which these activities or events have been inscribed, albeit implicitly, that the Award makes such a strong case for architecture as the setting for life, and hence the dictum and the title of this book, *Architecture Is Life*.

STEERING COMMITTEE BRIEF

The Award has an open perspective that promotes architectural projects that contribute to the transformation of the quality of life for Muslim communities. The setting of these transformations can be either urban or rural, national or diasporic. Within these contexts, the Muslim *umma* represents a pluralistic coming together of diverse values. In a world where the freedom of cultural expression is increasingly challenged, the Award aims to identify positive modes of practice that enable Muslim communities to take on the challenges of global transformation. Furthermore, the Award seeks to enable emerging Muslim communities to negotiate their role within the multicultural context of their host countries. Architecture and design provide alternative opportunities for promoting understanding, respect and reconciliation.

In its 12th Cycle, the Award will be considering projects in many Muslim societies that are at a critical political juncture. The significance of Muslims within the transnational networks of commodity production and consumption, which are expanding in emerging economies, can also be explored. The impact of such developments on local communities has been enormous, with social changes often lagging behind economic development. The impact, however, has not been uniform. Consequently, issues of equity, sustainability, scalability and good governance have become key factors that affect architecture and the built environment. But what is the effect of architecture on equitable governance? The Master Jury is urged to take these factors into consideration as part of its deliberations.

The Award is committed to the promotion of innovative responses to the built environment while recognising the importance of traditional methods and forms of architecture. The Award proposes an integrated approach that works towards the utilisation of best practices. In addition to architecture, master planning, landscape architecture and other modes of addressing and managing urban development, public transportation and infrastructure are high priorities for the Award. Of equal importance are places of work, sites for industrial production, public spaces, residential sectors, and spaces of retail and leisure. This interpretation of the built environment must also place a high premium on the issues of economic opportunity that profoundly affect the welfare and security of vulnerable people and communities.

In the context of these conditions, it is necessary to consider projects both for their overall architectural excellence and for the way they contribute to emerging paradigms for places of work, planning conditions, public spaces, housing and spaces of domesticity, health and welfare, conservation and adapted reuse.

In addition, it would be desirable to consider the following criteria: excellence in design, workmanship and craft, risk and reliance, sustainable practices, resource management, community activism, innovative governance and specific forms and manifestations of technical knowledge.

While it seems unlikely that any individual project fulfils all the above criteria, we hope that the projects premiated by the Master Jury will exemplify the historic and enduring aspiration of the Aga Khan Award for Architecture. This aspiration remains the understanding of, and appreciation for, the contributions that the built environment makes to the enhancement of the quality of life.

Excerpts from the Steering Committee brief to the 2013 Master Jury

REPORT OF THE MASTER JURY
The 2013 Cycle of the Aga Khan Award for Architecture

Contemporary Muslim communities live in contexts defined by large-scale movements and constantly negotiated notions of identity and homeland. These processes lead to an ongoing understanding of Self and Other, making for different combinations of volatility and creativity. The 2013 Jury was committed to identifying, acknowledging and awarding initiatives with the potential of helping communities negotiate challenges at multiple intersections, whether of historical time or space, or of the articulation of heritage with modernity. The dominant themes that define this cycle of awards are: restoration, as the revitalisation and adaptation of tradition; integration, as a way to unify fragmented environments, urban and rural; the pursuit of excellence in design in low-budget settings; and the embrace of the solemn dignity of death as a way to affirm life and the living.

Restoration often leads to the "museification" of spaces and artefacts as so many relics of a past gone by. The assumption is that tradition is something clinically separated from the present. The effect is, further, to ossify the past and disconnect it from the present. Where the immediate history of the peoples is concerned – in this case Muslim communities whose immediate past is anchored in colonised societies where the project of modernity was introduced as part of a foreign "civilising mission" – the damage is even greater. The Jury seeks to identify and acknowledge initiatives that highlight heritage as both alive and flexible, thereby affirming its potential as a resource that can invest the present with meaning. The objective is to make it possible for a people to take ownership of their history as a living tradition.

Restoration is never simply a return to the original. Among the projects the Jury awarded are those that highlight the potential of restoration to integrate a fragmented present. If in one instance the challenge is to let a community take ownership of its past, in another it is to unify a landscape fragmented by the confluence of multiple developments, official and unofficial. Muslim communities live in diverse environments, urban and rural. When it comes to village-based populations, the challenge is to validate the rural environment. Here, restoration is more than just about design; it calls for a participatory process and holistic approach that is greater than the sum of its parts.

Architecture is a quintessentially urban activity that is identified with urbanism and urban life. In spite of their density, urban settlements often generate an experience of solitariness, a feeling of being cut off in a disintegrated world. In a context where big bridges tend to be destructive elements within the city structure and the landscape, a bridge that touches the ground lightly and seeks to create places for pedestrian activity stands out. The bridge connects society, both metaphorically and physically, and contributes to a threefold integration: of public design, infrastructure and landscape.

Is it possible for a low-budget project to combine functionality with design, utility with beauty, affordability with excellence? Can architecture, historically a human activity highly destructive of the environment, take a posture that combines a low profile with high innovation, one that enables low-energy use alongside a recycling of resources? Among the projects the Jury acknowledges is that of a construction that turns decommissioned containers, a consumer culture waste product, into an aesthetically pleasing, low-cost building material, able to be used to provide much-needed health facilities and a high level of care to patients.

Rapid movement makes for a changing composition of communities, ethnic and religious. Questions around definitions, of home and away, self and other, have the potential of unleashing divisive tendencies. When an architectural intervention turns this volatility into an occasion for a sober and focused reflection, on life rather than death, it has the potential of giving the living a second chance. The Jury honours the grace and beauty of one such intervention, and its inclusiveness and foresightedness.

The Jury followed a two-step process in making its selection. The first step, which led to a shortlist of 20 projects, was based on identification of themes and challenges faced by practitioners of the built environment today. The second step was based on a threefold consideration – a holistic participatory approach, the quality of design, and its socio-economic-environmental impact – which led to the final selection of five worthy projects for the Aga Khan Award for Architecture:

– Salam Centre for Cardiac Surgery, Khartoum, Sudan
– Revitalisation of Birzeit Historic Centre, Palestine
– Rehabilitation of Tabriz Bazaar, Iran
– Rabat-Salé Urban Infrastructure Project, Morocco
– Islamic Cemetery, Altach, Austria.

Mahmood Mamdani (Chair), David Adjaye, Howayda al-Harithy, Michel Desvigne, Kamil Merican, Toshiko Mori, Shahzia Sikander, Murat Tabanlıoğlu, Wang Shu

THE PARTICULAR AND THE UNIVERSAL
Mahmood Mamdani

"I have a different idea of a universal. It is of a universal rich with all that is particular, rich with all the particulars there are, the deepening of each particular, the coexistence of them all."
Aimé Césaire (1957)[1]

Maoni is a Swahili word meaning points of view. The point of view of a jury is the result of a process. To convey a sense of that process is to sum up the key debates that shaped it. Every jury meets in a unique set of circumstances and faces a unique set of challenges. The central debate in this Jury unfolded around the question: who qualifies to compete for this Award? Should the project conform to some set of Islamic values, or an Islamic sensibility? Do the practitioners have to be Muslims? Do their clients or beneficiaries have to be Muslims? Do Muslims have to be living in the community where the project is sited? If so, how do we define the community? Is it the town, the province, the country? The debate can reach absurd levels, but the debate is not absurd. Central to it is the self-understanding of Muslims and of the understanding of Muslims as others.

MUSLIMS AND TRADITION
The question was brought to the forefront in the very first round of discussion. Should we be concerned with Islam or with Muslims? Should our concern be with doctrine or existence, with beliefs or lived reality? In this kind of formulation, what is at stake? It is worth focusing on key terms in this discussion — Islam and Muslims; culture, belief and lived reality — for one reason: the debate within the Jury reflected a debate outside the Jury, in wider society. Though the debate is not new, it has raged with particular ferocity since the event we know as 9/11.

In the weeks that followed 9/11, the American press was full of reports that increasing numbers of Americans were going to bookshops to buy copies of the Qur'an. These readers hoped the Qur'an would highlight the motivation of those who hijacked the planes, and rammed them into the Twin Towers. Soon *The New York Times* was telling us that the Qur'an was one of the highest-selling books in American bookshops. As the weeks rolled by there came the American invasion of Afghanistan and then, within months, the invasion of Iraq. It was public knowledge that the US President claimed to have a direct connection with God and claimed to be inspired. Why were Afghanis and Iraqis not seeking to read the Bible for a clue as to why America was bombing them? I wondered why the difference.

The nature of the public debate in the United States suggested a clue. Its contours were sketched by key intellectuals like Samuel Huntington at Harvard University and Bernard Lewis at Princeton University. Though these Ivy League icons were known to be on opposite sides in the public debate, their real importance was that they defined the common ground in that debate. That common ground came to be translated into "common sense", not only in the United States but also in much of the world outside its borders. This contemporary common sense did not stand on arbitrary ground; it has an unmistakable resemblance to assumptions that undergirded the colonial project in the modern era: that there is an absolute difference between the West and the rest, one that can only be bridged through a "civilising mission" aimed at conversion. Then, Africans were said to be the most extreme manifestation of that difference; in the period that followed 9/11, Muslims have come to occupy that position in the official Western imagination.

Contemporary common sense has it that you can read the politics of Muslims from their culture. In some writings, the difference between Muslims and others has come to resemble a caricature. It is said that modern culture is about creativity; that creativity is said to be historical; modern people are said to have a self-reflexive attitude to their culture; they have the capacity to separate the good from the bad, to build on the good and correct the bad, and thus develop their culture; that, in short, is the story of modern progress. The pre-modern stands in sharp contrast to the modern capacity to create culture. That contrast is said to be at its sharpest when it comes to Muslims, who are said to lack this capacity: except for a founding prophetic moment and some monuments, Muslims are said to be born into a cultural prison; they live their culture like a destiny; they wear culture as a badge, suffer it like a twitch, maybe a desert fever or a tropical fever; rather than an agent-driven historical process, Muslims are condemned to live their culture as so many targets, who have little choice but to pass this fate from one generation to another.

This caricature has a practical consequence. Instead of focusing on Muslims in the world, it promotes a focus on Muslims as a closeted group. Instead of promoting a reflection on inter-group relations, it seeks explanations of inter-group conflict in the doctrinaire posture of one particular group. The problem lies not so much with the notion of culture as it does with the idea that the culture of some peoples is historical and of others not. The alternative is to think of all cultures, including Islamic tradition, as constantly changing.

MUSLIMS IN THE WORLD
As the focus of attention shifted from doctrine to practitioners, from texts to community, a new set of questions arose. One, is the community to be understood as a special kind of community, a community of faith, a community constituted around the acceptance of certain core beliefs? Two, what about multi-faith communities, or plural communities whose residents either

practice or simply acknowledge adherence to different faiths? How important is it as to how many Muslims live in the community or how far Muslims live from where the project is situated?

The Muslim *umma*, the community, is a historical phenomenon. It is not an ahistorical given. Like any other people, Muslims are a historical people. True, there are individual states that today claim an Islamic identity, but the Islamic community is not identical with any particular state. Also true that there are individual countries where Muslims constitute an overwhelming majority of the population, yet the trend since the birth of Islam has been for Muslims to live in increasingly multi-faith communities. If this was mainly a product of conversion in an earlier period, it is today as much a product of migration as of conversion. In the contemporary world, it is difficult to think of any country that does not have Muslims as part of its citizenry. On the one hand, the *umma* is a trans-state community; on the other, it is enmeshed in a multi-faith community in each state.

Like any community, it is constituted through a duality of relations, internal and external. Internally, the Muslim *umma* is a community without a political centre. Culturally, too, it is multi-centred: to begin with, the Muslim *umma* is multilingual. Though we may say that the *umma* is a community of belief, the single most important fact about the Muslim *umma* is that it is a plural community, not just politically and culturally, but also spiritually. Defined by a plural existence, the *umma* gives rise to and is inspired by a plural sensibility.

Should the Aga Khan Award for Architecture be narrowly defined as a Muslim award or should it be broadly inspired by an Islamic sensibility? Should the Award be restricted to acknowledging specifically Islamic forms of the built environment, or should it seek to be as inclusive as possible, extending its acknowledgement to even those forms of the built environment that promote a sensibility Muslims would embrace, even if its origin or its contemporary identity is not explicitly Islamic?

The difference is one of point of view, *maoni*. It is most easily understood as the difference between two extreme views, one inward-looking, seeking preservation – even if at the risk of isolation – as its primary task, and the other outward-looking, seeking to prioritise dynamic engagement over preservation. An inward-looking orientation may be promoted from two different, even contradictory, points of view. It may be advanced from a position of self-defence, when a community under threat and at risk embraces a *laager*-type solution, as did Afrikaners in an earlier era. Or it may be advanced by those, Muslims or not, who seek to turn Islamic civilisation or environments that partake of an Islamic sensibility – in the vocabulary of the Chicago historian Thomas Hodgkin, Islamicate environments – into so many museumised collections. Not surprisingly, such an orientation often brings together constituencies with contradictory motives: on the one hand, those who are inspired by the enduring grace and beauty of historical sites and the endurance of communities that inhabit these and, on the other, those who are comforted by what they see as no more than unthreatening collections of lifeless artefacts and communities drained of life. If the former seeks to preserve life, the second seeks to mummify it.

An outward-looking orientation is more the result of a confident orientation that seeks to engage with the world as a realm of possibilities. It stands in sharp contrast to the risk-averse orientation that sees the environment as a constant source of dangers, including domination. The two orientations have rather different effects: an outward-looking orientation leads to a practice of inclusion, the inward orientation breeds exclusion. One tends to integration, the other to isolation. If the former point of view sees in integration the possibility of leadership, the latter sees in it the danger of a loss of identity.

The challenge for those who live in plural communities is not simply to promote an Islamic sensibility as an ongoing creative influence on the built environment, but also to see the world through the eyes of neighbours or others in doing so. If architecture is about building bridges, whether as reconciliation or as outreach, and not just about looking at isolated projects, then an award that seeks to live up to this challenge needs to go beyond a focus on Muslims only to one that acknowledges neighbours, beyond Islamic history to a broader history – one whose focus is not just Muslims looking inwards, but Muslims in the world.

Discussions on identity seldom close with an agreement. To put it differently, any agreement is provisional and tentative, marked by an understanding that its threads may be picked up, at another time and in a different place. Without muffling differences internal to the discussion, the Jury arrived at an implicit agreement on the terms of reference that would knit our deliberations: taking as our reference not Islam but Muslims, not as much defined by a faith or a doctrine but as the *umma*, whose lived reality is defined by plural understandings of Islam, dogmatic and libertine, doctrinaire and secular.

THE RURAL AND THE URBAN
Any person aged 40 and above – and this I think includes all members of the Jury – is aware that among pressing concerns put forward by contemporary youth is the call for a more holistic understanding of the environment, one that would lead to sustainability. As this shared concern evolves into a paradigm, it stresses custodianship of the environment over individual ownership and over an individual right to dispose privately held resources.

Historically, architecture has been a quintessentially urban practice. The story of development and progress, and indeed of universalism, has often been written as the culmination of a series of world-historical contexts that pit nomadic against sedentary peoples, and rural ways of life against a triumphant urbanity. One narrative that stands out in this account, because it challenges its linearity, is the story of the Mongol invasions of Europe and Asia.

The Mongols were no more than a million in the 12th century. Over the next hundred years, Genghis Khan, and then his sons and grandsons, conquered the most densely populated civilisations on earth, stretching from Siberia to India, Vietnam to Hungary, Korea to the Balkans. It was an empire larger than the one acquired by the Romans over 400 years.

Rather than see the empire of the Khans as no more than a cataclysmic wave of destruction wrought on the most advanced citadels of civilisation of that time – they burnt Kiev to the ground in 1240 and sacked Baghdad, the city of Sheherazade, the legendary teller of the *Arabian Nights*, in 1258 – it is worth seeing the ways in which this nomadic and rural challenge to urbanity was different. It is true that Europeans of the 19th century wrote of Mongols as barbarians motivated by lust and greed, but that is not how Europeans of the early Renaissance – such as Chaucer in the *Canterbury Tales* – wrote of Genghis Khan.

The Great Khan taught his troops to emphasise speed and surprise over fortifications and heavy armour, movement over built environments. The Khans founded no new religion, but championed religious freedom wherever they ruled. They financed the building of Christian churches in China, Qur'anic schools in Russia and Buddhist temples in Persia. Without being anti-religious, they became pioneers of a secular culture. Their form of "cosmopolitan universalism" gave us the Silk Road, then the largest free-trade area stretching across continents, and brought China and Europe into diplomatic and commercial contact for the first time in known history. The most important thing they built were bridges, crossing every river, lake and body of water they came across. Refusing to hold hostages, they pioneered the practice of granting diplomatic immunity across enemy boundaries. Even if they made no technological breakthrough, created no belief system, wrote few books, and refused to build castles and cities, the Mongols opened up the world to commerce, in goods and ideas, taking German miners to China and Chinese doctors to Persia, taking a metalworker from Paris to build a fountain in Mongolia, bringing the Chinese practice of fingerprinting to Persia, and spreading the use of carpets everywhere. Indeed, they made culture portable. In the words of Jack Weatherford, writing in *Genghis Khan and the Making of the Modern World*, the Mongol genius was "to turn the war of extinction into an amalgamation of cultures".

The principal beneficiaries of the Mongol invasions were Europeans, among the least developed peoples at the time. Although Mongols slaughtered the aristocratic knighthood of the continent, they were so disappointed by the general poverty of Europe that they bypassed its cities rather than looted them. Europe felt the destructive impact of the Mongol invasion through the incorporation of European prisoners into the Mediterranean slave trade: Mongol officers struck a deal with Italian merchants in the Crimea, selling European prisoners, especially young ones, as slaves around the Mediterranean. Merchants of Venice and Genoa set up trading posts in the Black Sea, and the Italians sold most of their slaves to the sultan of Egypt, who used them to create a slave army. With plenty of experience in fighting Mongols, this army of Slavs and Kipchaks, known as the Mamluks, finally defeated the Mongols at the Sea of Galilee in 1260.

The core victims of Mongol invasions included the most advanced regions and peoples of the time, among them Arabs. The classic Islamic text, which equates civilisation with urbanity and barbarism with rurality, Ibn Khaldun's *Muqaddimah*, needs to be situated in the aftermath of these invasions. Ibn Khaldun met Tamarlane in 1401, following the Great Khan's conquest of Damascus, and he wrote about it in some detail. Ibn Khaldun's intellectual influences came from two linguistic traditions, Arabic and Greek, in particular the Socratic tradition that equates civilisation with the *polis* and city life. But the socio-political-ideological context in which he wrote was very much informed by the consequences of the Mongol invasion. Writing a century after Genghis Khan and his nomadic forces had sacked Baghdad and decimated many an urban centre in the 13th century, Ibn Khaldun demonised three groups that he branded as not only outside urbanity but also antithetical to it: desert nomads (including the Berber and the Bedouin), cave-dwelling Slavs in the cold north, and forest "Negroes" south to the equator. Ibn Khaldun painted whatever stood outside the urban as devoid of civilisation. In doing so, he built on an existing tradition, arguably more Aristotelian than any other.

The Mongols were among the great carriers of culture to Europe, bringing to it the latest technology of the time (printing, firearms and the compass), introducing the wearing of new forms of dress (trousers and jacket which, compared to tunics and robes, made for easy mobility), a new style in painting pictures, and musical instruments based on the bow rather than plucking strings with fingers. They exemplify the opposite of assimilation: exchange. To return to the epigram with which this essay begins, when it comes to actually existing history, it is Mongols who, more than any other group of conquerors, sought to create "a universal rich with all that is particular, rich with all the particulars there are, the deepening of each particular, the coexistence of them all".

To rethink these relationships – between modernity and tradition, the urban and the rural – is in fact to rethink universalism itself. It is to contrast two different kinds of universalism in history. It is to see what is different about the Mongol case, with its focus on a relentless exchange between different parts of the empire. The real significance of the Mongol case is that it highlights a universalising tendency that is not the opposite of the particular, but a composite of particulars.

The city looms as the primary artefact in the history of human civilisations. It is the centre point of the architectural imagination. It is no exaggeration to say that when it comes to the Western tradition, the city has been synonymous with the human, and not just the modern. For Aristotle, the city was the home of civic virtues. For Max Weber, even though urbanisation was advanced in many parts of the non-Western world, "the Western city" stood as a unique phenomenon. The difference was this: kinship connections cut across the urban-rural divide in the non-Western world, thus ensuring that cities remained more embedded in the local agrarian economy; in contrast, "the Western city" of the post-medieval period was marked by a high level of political autonomy that set off "bourgeois" society from agrarian feudalism.

The history of architecture is part of the larger history of the urban. If architecture has brought order, beauty and grace to the urban environment, it has also been at the cutting edge of an aggressive and colonising urbanism. This reflects the larger relationship between the rural and the urban. In the modern era, development has been another name for urbanisation. Very little thought has gone into the possibility of the rural developing on its own basis, or in a mutually beneficial relationship with the urban, one that would make for a sustainable development of the rural. On the contrary, the rural has been seen as the repository of a relatively static tradition, a drag on progress rather than a resource for it.

Contemporary notions of the rural as the harbinger of tradition and the urban as the springboard for the modern were crafted in the modern period, and have continued since. In large sections of the non-Western world, modernisation is synonymous with the urban colonising the rural. Only if we think that the roots of the modern lie outside the rural does it make sense to think of development as a process that can only be induced from the outside. For such a unidimensional imagination, modernisation is equivalent to the destruction of the rural. There is, of course, a counter-tendency that has stood apart from and even against such one-dimensional thinking, one that thinks of durable rural futures not in antagonism with but in a productive relationship with the urban. The real challenge is thus to think of different kinds of urbanisations, different types of relationships, each anchored in a different relationship between the urban and the rural, the coloniser and the colonised. The result is more of an integration, an interpenetration of different traditions, rather than just a one-way assimilation. Even when it comes to a context resembling a one-way process, one recalls Senghor's dictum to the Senegalese, faced with the French *mission civilisatrice*: "Assimilate, don't be assimilated!"

The contemporary rural stands out as different from its predecessors in one important respect. Its relationship with the urban has undergone one important shift: with the onset of the IT revolution, the rural is no longer as isolated from the urban. This is discernible, in particular, in the subjectivity of the young as the virtual world of the Internet gives an ever-larger shared sense to young people. With increasing connectivity between the rural and the urban and the emergence of new visual layers of meaning, neither villages nor villagers are as cut off from mainstream flows as hamlets and villages of yesteryears.

For practitioners of the built environment, this discussion should raise a question of balance, between different modes of living and different ways of appropriating and living in the environment. What would it mean to shift perspective from a top-down to a bottom-up approach when it comes to the transformation of the rural? Can those who specialise in design bring to country homes and community halls – made more often than not from modest materials starting with thatch and mud bricks – a durability and endurance that may have been lacking historically? If we are to think of traditional practices not just in terms of materials – thatch, mud – but also in terms of design, it should become possible to think of modernisation in both a plural and a bottom-up sense.

Philosophical critics of relentless human greed – from Tolstoy to Thoreau to Gandhi, from Rousseau to Fanon to Nyerere – have heralded the minimalist ethical and consumption practices of the rural and seen in these a surer guarantee of a human future, more secure than one promised by the overall greed and consumer culture that has come to characterise contemporary urbanity.

The implications for architects and architecture are clear. For those who understand architecture as a landscape rather than a building, the architectural lens needs to highlight drivers of social change and not just the excellence of design, shaping a focus that can extend beyond the present and highlight transitional processes, pointing to diverse futures and promoting diverse values of scale and sustainability. The challenge of sustainability raises a question: how can architecture relate to the countryside on different terms? How can it negotiate the social distance between the city and the country through an ethic of pluralism rather than one of conversion, seeking to acknowledge and build on how rural peoples live in particular environments? These understandings of the ethical, and of the good life, are equally relevant to Muslim-majority communities as to communities where Muslims are minorities, however small.

1 Aimé Césaire, *Letter to Maurice Thorez*, Paris: Présence Africaine, 1957.

GEOGRAPHY AND ARCHITECTURE
David Adjaye

This was my first experience with the Aga Khan Award for Architecture and I was impressed by the way in which the Jury discussion was organised. In these situations the emphasis is often on visual questions, but here we were provided with an in-depth analysis of each project. Based on people going into the field and interviewing stakeholders, users and members of the community, the On-Site Review gave a full technical breakdown of the building's strengths and innovations, and any areas where it might be less viable. This was really illuminating as it shifted our understanding to the question of how the projects contributed to the local community – with the imagery playing a supportive role, rather than dominating the discussion. As the Awards are for buildings that engage with the Muslim *umma,* they can have widely different functions and sizes, and be located almost anywhere in the world. The On-Site Reviews therefore played an important role in ensuring that we understood the terms of reference for each project.

The notion that architecture has the capacity to make sensitive contributions to a wide range of situations around the globe is one I have been increasingly drawn to. I have always been fascinated by the global mutations of modern architecture and this is the type of work that I am constantly being drawn back to. Whether in Japan, South America or India, modernism evolved in surprising ways as it encountered different cultural and climatic conditions from those in which it had first developed. The creative moment between a general model and a set of highly specific conditions is an opportunity for innovation, for questioning established scenarios and developing new models. This oscillation between a universal idea and a condition on the ground means that the work itself never becomes decoupled and self-contained: in the process of adapting to the location, it remains part of a wider discourse.

The connection between geography and architecture was one of the things I looked at in my book on the capital cities of Africa.[1] I decided to make the study because I felt that Africa was often seen as an exotic place that had become disconnected from the rest of the world, a troubled continent that had little to offer. Having been brought up there, I saw it rather differently, as a place where every possible variant had been produced and every relationship had been contested. Colonialism, for instance, is often assumed to have had similar consequences in different cities, which was neither the case at the time nor now – as they continue to develop. By immersing myself in the experience of the cities, I began to notice tendencies and patterns. Some examples seemed quite bizarre but, as I looked more closely, I could see how they responded to the conditions in different climatic zones. This was the basis for classifying all the cities according to their position in one of six "geographic zones", a term that is intended to suggest the interaction between a set of general conditions and a specific location.

In each city I photographed representative building types and made a record of what I saw in the streets and open spaces. The overview in the book is based on combining these images in a loose order, and can be understood in two different ways. As I collected the material in a relatively short period, it provides a record of the cities at a particular time and can, therefore, be used as a reference point for studying their future development. Showing buildings of different generations coming up to the present, and examples of recent informal developments, it also illustrates patterns of development that are likely to extend into the future. As the rate of urbanisation in Africa continues to rise, tracking these patterns will be an essential tool in developing strategies for the future of these cities.

The introductions to each of the geographic zones provide basic climatic data: temperature range, seasonal rainfall, and their effects on the vegetation and landscape. But once in the cities, I was more concerned with recording the human response to these conditions, whether in the formal architecture, vernacular buildings or the way in which external spaces were used. Rather than making a physical analysis, I wanted to understand the impact of climate on the lifestyle of the people, how they used place and occupied space in response to the prevalent conditions. My reading is that the way of life in these places is a precise response to the climate, and has as much architectural potential as any environmental technology. With the increasing use of air conditioning, it is worth remembering that many people will continue to live in an environment that was developed on a different basis. One of the strengths of the Salam Centre for Cardiac Surgery in Khartoum is the way that it acknowledges this reality.

Much of the vernacular building in Africa is a direct response to climate. In the traditional compound house, which now has descendants on many suburban plots, most domestic activities took place in the protected courtyard. The mud-brick houses of the Sahel have thick walls and small openings to protect the interior from the strength of the sun, and the houses in the forest zone have deep verandas for shade, and to shelter the external wall from torrential rain so that it can still be used for ventilation. More recently, the introduction of "tropical modernism" has seen a proliferation of larger buildings in which solar shading devices dominate the exterior at the expense of conventional doors and windows. In my photographs of these examples, I was interested in recording how they often succeeded in modifying the harsh light, sometimes in combination with landscape elements. The atmosphere they create is the first thing one experiences, and that is something I am very conscious of in the development of my own work.

The cultural phenomenon that most directly reflects my initial perception of the continent, as a place of many intersecting histories, is that of hybridisation. The main ethnic groups originally occupied fairly distinct areas but during the last millennium many of them migrated and interacted more frequently with other groups. This process has been accelerated by more recent contact with the outside world through slavery, colonialism and international developments in the post-colonial era. The effects of these movements in terms of hybridisation are widely reflected in the urban environment: cities with distinct quarters whose organisation stems from the culture of their original inhabitants; areas that have been abandoned by one population and reoccupied by another; eclectic combinations of buildings with different cultural sources; and buildings that mix indigenous and international motifs. Two of my favourite instances are the people of Asmara enjoying the *passeggiata* in the arcaded streets built by Italian colonisers, and the multi-faith skyline of Kampala, with the grand mosque, a Sikh *gurdwara,* and at least two cathedrals standing on separate hilltops.

I am interested in hybridisation as an indicator of cultural change, and in the possibility of including such elements in my own work to make it accessible to a wider audience. The design of the Smithsonian National Museum of African American History and Culture, which we are currently building in Washington DC, involves the introduction of a hybrid form, a crown-like superstructure, which is based on a Yoruba sculpture from Nigeria. Although it might appear to be an intrusion, it is intended to complement the existing buildings. As it happens, the motif of my building is already represented in the Washington Monument but, standing on its own, the Monument appears to be the exception to everything around it. By contextualising the Monument, we hope to show how the system represented by the other buildings on the Mall is not as autonomous as it first appears, and how it connects with other systems.

From the outside, Africa may look like a *tabula rasa*, the site of a long line of experiments that have little to do with each other, but closer acquaintance confirms that it is contested ground where the local conditions have been transformed by outside forces. This, too, has echoes in the wider world, where the effects of globalisation have undermined the identity of familiar places. In most of the situations I look at as an architect, many histories overlap and I try to avoid the temptation to draw out one of them at the expense of the others. Rather than responding to physical traces, I prefer to extrapolate the emotive conditions suggested by earlier narratives. These may involve creating a sense of denial, opportunity, reflection, aloofness or conviviality, which contributes to the atmosphere of the building – the device that first communicates what a building has to offer.

My desire to understand the attributes of African cities by classifying them in groups does not entirely recognise the nature of some of their differences.

Many of the capitals had strong international links earlier in their history, which have remained equally or more significant since independence. In the case of Accra, for instance, Nkrumah began to restructure the city in response to its new status as the capital of a republic that would play a significant role within Africa and on the world stage. The double orientation, inwards to the country and outwards to the rest of the globe, is a feature of many capital cities but is particularly legible in Africa, where the distances between the cities are so great. The orientation of the African examples, and the strength of their external connections, can make a significant difference to the identities of cities in the same geographic terrain. We are currently working in several African cities and most of our projects are intended to have a profile that will be meaningful when read from different distances. This fits with my concern that architecture should both address the nature of everyday experience and contribute to a wider discourse on the nature of habitation.

I am interested in moving away from a position where architecture is judged in terms of a single criterion of progress to one in which several scenarios can be considered at once. In this connection, I appreciated the way in which the On-Site Reviews, provided to the Award Jury, ensured the widest possible discussion of the shortlisted projects. Although it focuses on buildings that contribute to the Muslim experience, the Aga Khan Award for Architecture engages with the diffuse nature of contemporary practice, from the Rehabilitation of Tabriz Bazaar to the hybridity of a modernist Islamic Cemetery in Vorarlberg. This is why the concerns of the Award are relevant to all of us.

1 David Adjaye, *African Metropolitan Architecture*, New York, Rizzoli, 2011, also published as *Adjaye Africa Architecture*, London, Thames & Hudson, 2011.

INNOVATION AND JUDGEMENT
Toshiko Mori

My participation as a Jury member of the 12th Cycle of the Aga Khan Award for Architecture was unlike any of my other experiences. Through the lens of diverse activities of Muslim communities, one perceives the dynamic state of the world at large, presenting dilemmas, complexities, conflicts and resolutions.

Being on the Master Jury is a rigorous yet rewarding process. The criteria for the judgement must relate to the context, location, time, and both environmental and political climate. Unlike typical competitions or award juries where criteria parameters often lead to a clear direction or an identity of a jury, the projects kept us in constant flux by challenging our preconceptions. Through discussions and familiarisation with each of the submissions, a series of complex and thought-provoking questions emerged from the projects. Throughout the process, we maintained open-minded and discursive conversations, often departing from our personal comfort zones. This attitude was crucial for addressing the many projects that were sited in places of adversity and conflict, and often immersed in fluid circumstances. The members of the Jury came from a variety of backgrounds, arriving with a wide range of expertise, interests and cultural experiences, which contributed to a productive, energetic and healthy exchange of opinions.

The dominant themes in the projects were socially targeted, aiming to sustain, maintain or strengthen fragile communities in an ever-changing world. The solutions and innovations proposed in these projects addressed the importance of long-term, community survival, for a lasting impact on the global architectural context. The innovative ideas in these projects were a result of circumstances with scarce resources, encouraging creativity and inventive strategies. The innovations presented here were not necessarily something new in themselves, but, rather, involved clever re-contextualising or reconfiguration. Innovation took place as a lateral shift of context, instead of a vertical gear change, transforming familiar materials and methods into something pervasive and extraordinary.

A most fascinating aspect for this Jury was that the sites and programmes reflected the current state of the world at large, of locations ranging from the Middle East, Asia and Africa to Europe, allowing us to question the standards we often impose as the criteria for judging projects. The conventional notion that innovation must be an abrupt agent of change, often associated with social mobility, was put under scrutiny for projects that promoted small incremental steps to achieve a whole, a contingent strategy that can adjust more easily to a changing socio-political climate in volatile communities. We have come to understand that in order for the innovation to stay robust, it must begin in small steps, at a personal level, thereby providing opportunities for a larger-scale expansion. This outlook embraced by some NGOs is an inventive method of social stability. I would like to introduce five innovative examples that inspired the Master Jury of the 12th Cycle of the Award.

PARTICIPATORY PRACTICE:
THE COINCIDENCE OF PROCESS AND ARCHITECTURE
The historic architecture and urbanism of Tabriz Bazaar deserved recognition for its timeless and effective integration of structure and ornament, environmental responsiveness, and layout and circulation that promote urbanity and a balance between commercial and public activities. The rehabilitation was a grassroots-initiated process that embraced thoughtful and holistic principles of traditional ways of life in the Bazaar. The multidisciplinary nature of this process integrated economics with social structure and architecture, making this project a robust model for participatory practice of our time. While the structure of this society is traditional, contemporary society can learn a great deal from a bottom-up project, including initiation and long-term maintenance that involve a multitude of stakeholders that include 5000-plus merchants and government members.

The wonderful connection between architecture and this process is that both are interdependently organised in a rich and complex configuration. With the concept of inclusiveness, connectivity and engagement, both the Bazaar and the community became self-sustaining entities. The participatory process extended to the materials and technique of this project, as local materials and skills reflected the traditional quality of the place. Furthermore, it included interventions that allowed this historical place to adapt to future innovations and contemporary society, and demonstrated the notion of historic preservation as an act of social contract. Here, history becomes a dynamic vehicle for citizens' everyday lives. The initiative created a collective sense of ownership and stewardship. It is a monumental project not only because of its scale, but also because of the effort of rehabilitation and its ongoing commitment to revitalise a fragile place.

INNOVATION THROUGH TYPOLOGICAL HYBRIDISATION
The Rabat-Salé Urban Infrastructure Project in Morocco uses a bridge as the primary building typology to address complex issues such as mobility, transportation, socio-economics and ecology. It includes an analysis of the properties of the Bridge's function, its capacity to connect as well as to divide, extend as well as to fuse, and to differentiate the two sides of the Bridge. The project takes advantage of the multidimensional aspects of infrastructure, maximising its responsiveness on all of the exposed and occupied surfaces.

The Hassan II Bridge was minimised where it spans the Bouregreg River, but maximised for a gradual transition into the neighbourhood on both sides. The space below the Bridge is over-scaled in height, anticipating future public functions, such as markets or public gathering spaces. The space enables two edges of divided land to connect and give access to the waterfront from the landside. The asymmetrical treatment of the land on both sides of the Bridge reflects the different sociologies of Rabat and Salé. Another interesting characteristic of this project is that although the proposed hybrid bridge has an iconic presence, it does not convey this through a monumental or sculptural gesture. Instead, it is deferential to landscape and other civic monuments. The Bridge carries different modes of transportation such as a motorway, tramway and pedestrian paths, and is divided into three decks. Instead of a larger and heavier structure, subdivided decks are thinner and more elegant, with a gap that also provides daylight into the space below the Bridge.

The Bridge is a progressive and responsive hybridised gradation of an arched main bridge to the viaduct on the Salé side, and a nautical bridge on the Rabat side. The structural language is altered to suit the programmes and geography on either embankment, creating a bridge that merges gracefully into the horizon. The Bridge is intentionally suppressed in height to avoid disrupting the flat and horizontal landscape of the site. This approach to bridge design, somewhat counter-intuitive for conventional bridge designs, succeeded by being responsive to its site and context.

INCREMENTAL INTERVENTION STRATEGY
The Revitalisation of Birzeit Historic Centre is unique in that it recognises the importance of the "in between spaces" that define Palestinian statehood, as well as addresses the incremental creation of public spaces. Instead of restoring individual buildings, the project focuses on the rural vernacular architectural "connective tissues" and circulatory systems to create continuous and cumulative impact. Riwaq, which concentrates its efforts on upgrading infrastructure, street paving and rehabilitation, calls it a "preventive conservation". There is also an emphasis on the rehabilitation of the historic urban fabric, and key buildings that are the generators of work and life of the community. The innovative idea presented here is the redefinition of preservation as an entire fabric, which goes beyond an artefact and its historical significance. It creates a larger-format precondition for a longer-term, incremental implementation.

The project recreates a powerful narrative of heritage for the community, empowering it with a new identity and viable future. These results can be applied elsewhere, as proposed by Riwaq's "50 Villages" initiative to revitalise rural communities in Palestine, where 90% of the population lives. This concept can contribute to the solution to balance rural communities and rapidly growing urban centres throughout the world. Their process is focused, based on conceptual clarity.

REPURPOSE THROUGH NESTING AND LAYERING
The Salem Centre for Cardiac Surgery presents the clever appropriation technique of existing building systems for new use that allowed for fast and cost-effective responses. The innovation lies in the way in which these basic building models are repurposed with minimal and decisive design decisions. The hospital block consists of two standard building systems that nest one inside the other and create a service plenum, which also conceals an otherwise intimidating apparatus of hospital machinery. This cavity also helps to mitigate extreme heat from the clinical and ward areas. This simple strategy enabled the architects to build high-quality cardiac surgery units. The medical staff area is housed in out-of-commission containers, to which both external and internal panels were added as layers to achieve environmental comfort in response to the harsh climate of Khartoum.

The project utilises economical and accessible materials, but the design is focused on detailing the places critical to human experience and performance. This strategy is not only an innovative, universal approach to architecture, but is also astounding in that its world-class quality, standard of excellence, and beauty is achieved in such a difficult place. The project achieves poetic presence through a clear vision, without compromising excellence.

INNOVATION IN THE NUANCED USE OF ARCHITECTURAL LANGUAGE
In terms of the use and appropriation of architectural language, the Islamic Cemetery in Altach, Austria, is a thoughtful and careful invention, combining contemporary, local architectural language with an unusual function. The contemporary architecture of this location has a minimalist expression and disciplined severity. The horizontal and stretched siting technique contrasts with the dominant and picturesque mountainous landscape, allowing for a wilful, yet subtle intervention. In its articulation and ornamentation, the architecture combines Islamic motifs crafted in the local Voralberg tradition. This uncanny interweaving of cultures and references makes us question the larger meaning of "homeland", and allowed the Jury to consider a new formation of architectural language in a world in which we are experiencing an increased rate of migration.

These are some examples of innovative practice observed during the Jury deliberation process. Innovation is often associated with disruption and acceleration, social mobility, productivity and economic gain. Yet these examples are brought about through careful and collaborative thought processes, which overcome obstacles and permeate vast layers of society, there-fore contributing to stabilisation and cohesion. The lesson here is to consider innovation as an interwoven fabric of society that redefines the recipient from a selected few to a larger populace. Instead of productivity, innovation addresses empowerment and, in lieu of economic gain, innovation delivers benefits.

THE AWARD AND CHINA
Wang Shu

Some Chinese architects were already familiar with the Aga Khan Award for Architecture back in the early 1980s. At that time, China was just beginning to open up to the world after a long period of closure. Chinese architects had little knowledge about other architectural awards in the world. I think the reason why Chinese architects were interested in the Aga Khan Award was because the premiated projects presented an effort to combine modern Western architectural language with vernacular architectural concepts, which, at the time, interested many Chinese architects. From the perspective of today, these efforts were serious and sincere.

In the early 1980s, the Award collaborated with the Architectural Society of China to organise an academic gathering to discuss rural habitat. In the first decade of the 21st century, the large-scale urbanisation of China's countryside was approaching, and the discussion points of that seminar are still relevant today as they referred to the research for sustainable development. What is more important, the countryside building activities that the Award is concerned with are mostly bottom-up participatory efforts that consider the general community to be the main actor. Though the effort seems to be fragmentary, in the Internet era, attention to these projects represents a positive tendency of resistance to the hegemony of modernisation in urban and rural planning and the assertive way of construction.

ENDLESS INVENTIVENESS
Shahzia Sikander

As a visual artist, what inspired me most about being a member of the Master Jury for the 12th Cycle of the Aga Khan Award for Architecture was the lack of any culturally specific lens throughout the process. There was no intent to champion a solely Islamic context or valorise an Islamic aesthetic. It was, in fact, an emphasis on originality that preceded all concerns: originality as located within the creative responses to a set of unique problems.

As values are discerned within the built environment, the need to reflect and question what can be improved and addressed differently becomes a necessary dialogue. The needs that dictate reinterpreting the existing norms are often a catalyst for new ways of arriving at a solution. Such active engagement is also necessary in defining the larger context of Islamic art and architecture. Muslim communities have varied histories and geographical locations that challenge singular definitions. Furthermore, in today's transnational ways of living and being, the older frameworks feel increasingly restrictive. Inherently nationalistic sentiments remain strong even in art history. The quest to define an Islamic identity in the contemporary visual context may be a paradox in itself. Though it has been laboured upon and often reduced to a cliché, its potential remains strong, since fundamental values of inclusiveness and plurality lie at its core.

Art, and especially architecture, interfere and interact with the social, political and economic changes in a society. At these cross roads lie artistic interventions that, when harnessed to unique visions, independent from their historical representations, encourage others to experiment, explore and expand upon the notion of an inherited form. In fact, there lies the challenge: to conceive and imagine an aesthetic that is inclusive and a reflection of a community's unique relationship to its local environment.

CRAFT

What are the benefits of the knowledge gained from mastering the art of making things? Projects such as the Preservation of the Mbaru Niang, Kantana Film and Animation Institute and Mapungubwe Interpretation Centre all rely on the understanding of use and shape of materials. The specific nature of this knowledge is based on repetition and precedence. But the capacity for innovation is always implicit in the elasticity of the knowledge of the craftsman and of a specific craft.

PRESERVATION OF THE MBARU NIANG
Wae Rebo Village, Flores Island, Indonesia

Wae Rebo is a remote village settled 17 generations ago (according to oral tradition), located deep within mountainous rainforest in the Manggarai area on the island of Flores in eastern Indonesia. The site is a grassy plateau some 1200 metres above sea level and is only accessible on foot. In the late 1960s, a development programme under the Suharto government forcibly relocated other nearby villages to the lowlands, pulling down traditional housing in the process. But the Wae Rebo community remained in its isolated site and successfully retained its traditional conical houses of "worok" wood, bamboo and thatch, known as *mbaru niang*, standing some 13 metres high. As symbols of unity in the family and community, these dwellings are the communal domestic and ceremonial space for an entire clan, sheltering up to eight families (35–45 people), their crops, food and ritual belongings over five storeys.

In 2008, a group of young Jakarta-based architects on a study trip to Flores arrived to find four – out of an original seven – of these houses remaining, two of which were in need of rebuilding. Eager to preserve this last example of Manggarai vernacular building, and in so doing the Wae Rebo culture and way of life, the architects initiated and facilitated the community-led renovation, but only after traditional skills lost over time had been relearnt by the community in reverse during the dismantling process of the older structures.

After this was successfully completed, the project expanded to rebuild three more *mbaru niang* on the footprint of the earlier houses, restoring the village to its original state of seven houses arranged in a U-shape around a simple open-air altar. All the materials are natural and were sourced locally, and the community provided all the labour, learning on the job.

A central column rises through the elaborate multi-storey frame in hardwood, braced by four diagonals that define the conical shape; the floors are tied into the structure and the whole is covered almost to ground level by bamboo and thatch. The ground-floor living area is divided by the central post into reception area at the front and cooking to the rear, with perimeter cubicles acting as bedrooms. The four upper storeys are for storage and ritual spaces.

PRESERVATION OF THE MBARU NIANG
Wae Rebo Village, Flores Island, Indonesia

CLIENT AND BUILDER
Wae Rebo Community, Flores Island, Indonesia:
Martinus Anggo, project leader and community representative
Fransiskus Mudir, construction manager
Alexander Ngadus, Isidorus Ingkul, Thomas Pakur, supervisors

PROJECT COORDINATOR
Rumah Asuh, Jakarta, Indonesia:
Yori Antar, founder
Varani Kosasih, Paskal Khrisno Ayodyantoro, project managers
Robin Hartanto, Faiz Hamdi Suprahman, Ronaldiaz Hartantyo, Adi Reza Nugroho, Arya Wisnu Wardhana, students

PROJECT DATA
Site area: 6500 m^2
Footprint of each house: 101 m^2
Total combined floor area: 1005 m^2
Cost: 206,000 USD
Study: August–December 2008
Construction: May–October 2009 (phase 1); February–May 2010 (phase 2); November 2010–May 2011 (phase 3)
Completion: May 2011

RUMAH ASUH
Rumah Asuh, meaning "foster house", is a Jakarta-based team of architects. The members of this team ordinarily work within the commercial practice of Han Awal & Partners, and, under the mentorship of the architect Yori Antar, Rumah Asuh also works voluntarily to understand, document and help preserve some of the endangered indigenous architectural traditions of Indonesia.
The collective was born out of the experience of the trip of 15 young Jakarta-based architects and students to the remote village of Wae Rebo in 2008. Back in Jakarta, the group – later to be known as Rumah Asuh – remained motivated to assist the Wae Rebo community. The conservation of Wae Rebo is their first on-site project. During the rebuilding phases, students on on-site placements actively participated in the construction through Rumah Asuh and became responsible for documenting, through different media, the entire rebuilding process.

KANTANA FILM AND ANIMATION INSTITUTE
Nakhon Pathom, Thailand

Massive eight-metre-high, undulating brick walls distinguish the Kantana Film and Animation Institute that was set up by the Kantana Group, one of the largest film and animation production companies in Thailand, to offer undergraduate studies in filmmaking and animation for aspiring filmmakers.

The Institute is located in the town of Klong Yong in Nakhon Pathom province, some 56 kilometres from the capital Bangkok, in an open rural site of grasslands and paddy fields. Enclosed within their rippling brick walls pierced by irregularly placed square openings, the five main functional areas of the complex – lecture hall, library, studio-workshops, administration and canteen – are arranged around two prominent intersecting, open-air, cobbled walkways. Planted with 10- to 20-metre-high Peeb trees, these walkways are called "inserted forests" by the architect, keen to blend architecture and nature – the main inspiration for the design and a direct reference to Thai culture. These wide walkways run centrally east-west and north-south through the layout, allowing efficient pedestrian circulation and connections, good ventilation and additional natural shade, interesting plays of light effects, and areas for quiet meditation and inspiration in their window-seating niches.

The monumental walls – the hallmark of the project – called for over 600,000 handmade bricks which were made one by one from the soil of the site, reviving not only a traditional building material and technique but also a declining local factory, while creating jobs for 100 brick makers from two neighbouring villages. The bricks were laid in a staggered fashion to create the spectacular recessions and protrusions of the double-layer walls, internally supported on a steel frame: the double layer creating an air space providing insulation from the tropical heat. The careful siting of windows, insertion of inner courtyards in the quadrangles, abundance of new planting in the immediate surroundings and two water features also aid cooling and the quality of light entering the interiors. Within its brick walls, the building stands on a reinforced-concrete post-and-beam frame system (a prevalent construction system in the province) and partition walls are hollow concrete: a successful blend of modern materials – concrete and steel – with an extraordinarily innovative use of Thailand's traditional brickwork, as seen in the stepped and banded work on brick temples.

The project has undoubtedly triggered a renewed interest on the part of Thai architects in brickwork.

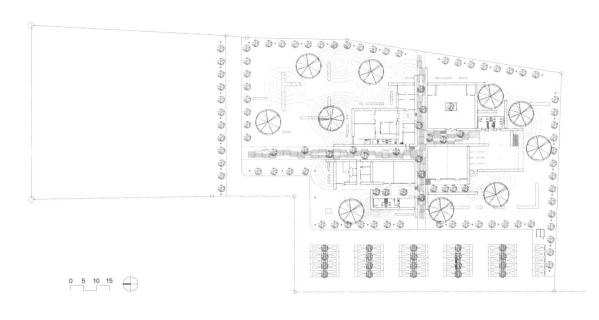

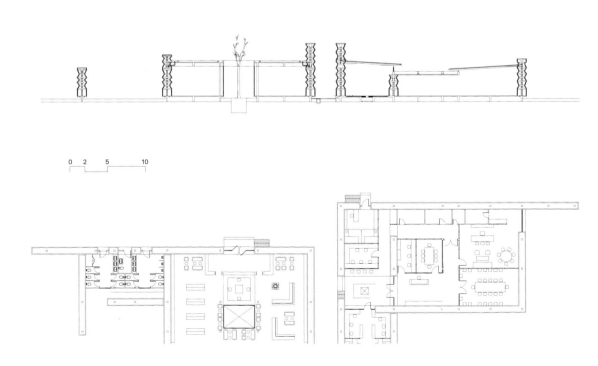

KANTANA FILM AND ANIMATION INSTITUTE
Nakhon Pathom, Thailand

CLIENT
Kantana Group Public Company, Bangkok, Thailand:
Jareuk Kaljareuk, chairman

ARCHITECT
Bangkok Project Studio, Bangkok, Thailand:
Boonserm Premthada, founder
Ittidej Lirapirom, Piiyasak Mookmaenmuan, project team

STRUCTURAL ENGINEER
Preecha Suvapabkul, Bangkok, Thailand

MECHANICAL AND SANITARY SYSTEM ENGINEER
Tanete Chaiyaphong, Bangkok, Thailand

ELECTRICAL ENGINEER
Wittaya Nakasan, Bangkok, Thailand

CONTRACTOR
Deco Decorate and System, Bangkok, Thailand

BRICK MANUFACTURER
BBK Brick Factory, Angthong Province, Thailand

PROJECT DATA
Site area: 16,000 m^2
Ground-floor area: 2000 m^2
Cost: 1,000,000 USD
Commission: March 2006
Design: March 2006–June 2009
Construction: August 2009–June 2011
Completion: June 2011

BOONSERM PREMTHADA
Born in Bangkok, Thailand, Boonserm Premthada graduated in 2003 with a Master of Architecture degree from Chulalongkorn University and went on to establish his own practice, Bangkok Project Studio, in 2004. Boonserm's approach is one of adventurousness and artistic daring, particularly in the application of atmosphere. His design-creation approach to human sensation and the touch of nature uses diverse criteria: connectedness to place, appropriate use of local materials and technology, and cultivation of environment. His ideal focus is on the phenomena of atmosphere, such as silence, slowness, meditation, dimness and timelessness. In addition, his works are a reflection of social responsibility and improve the quality of life by adopting self-sufficient strategies.
At present, besides working as an architect and artist, Boonserm also lectures at the Faculty of Architecture of Chulalongkorn University.

WEBSITE
www.kantanainstitute.ac.th/en/home

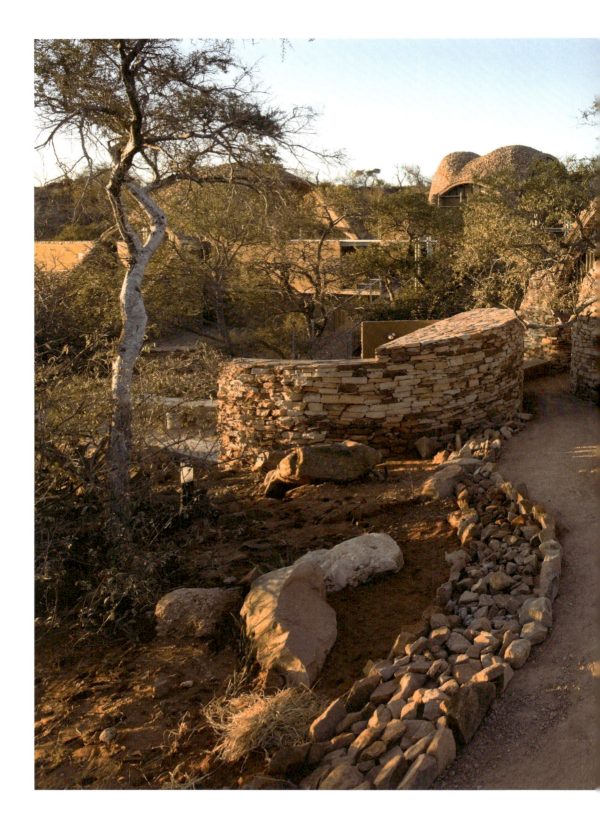

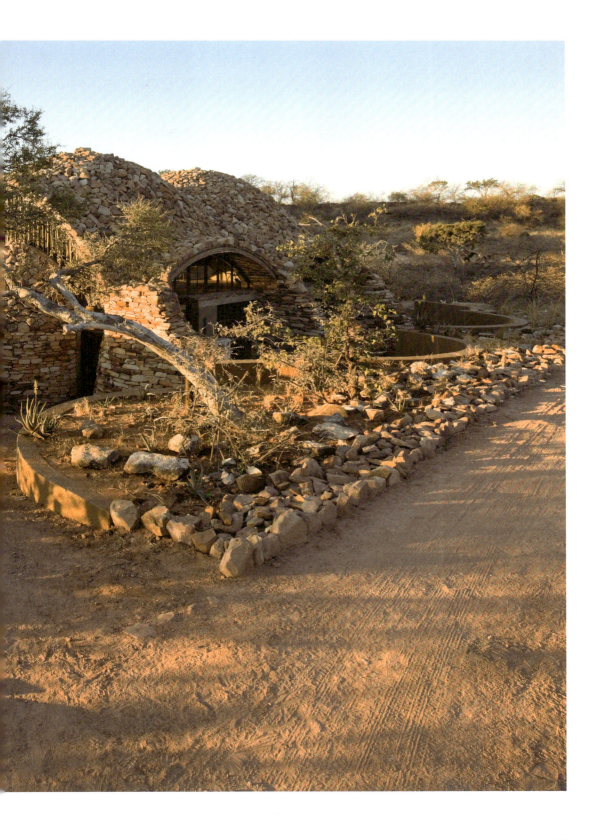

MAPUNGUBWE INTERPRETATION CENTRE
Limpopo Province, South Africa

Mapungubwe Interpretation Centre stands in the rocky landscape of the Mapungubwe National Park located in the remote and isolated Limpopo Valley, which is in the north of South Africa at the point where South Africa, Zimbabwe and Botswana meet. The Park celebrates the ancient trading civilisation of Mapungubwe, a kingdom that flourished between the 11th and 14th centuries and that produced such artefacts as the famed Golden Rhino. The site was discovered in 1933 and listed as a World Heritage Site in 2003, which provided the impetus for developing Mapungubwe, with the Interpretation Centre a natural consequence of this.

To fulfil its objectives, the Centre comprises a museum with a series of linked exhibition halls and visitor facilities, as well as offices for the Park staff, an outdoor amphitheatre and facilities for researchers. It is sited alongside a flat-topped, steep-sided hill, or mesa, that sisters the main mesa of the site, the ceremonial centre of the Mapungubwe civilisation, one kilometre away.

In designing the Centre, architect Peter Rich was inspired by the spectacular semi-arid scenery of the sandstone outcrops dotted with huge baobab and mopane trees in the surrounding hilly savannah. These elements of nature inform the series of vaulted forms, laid in a triangular arrangement up the hillside and linked by outside areas and bridges in a combination of "ins and outs" that make up a complex of structures that are authentically rooted to their location.

The thin-shell, double curvature vaults, barrel vaults and domes – the most visible architectural element of the design, especially when lit up at night – span up to 14.5 metres and revive a centuries-old technique that relies on fast-setting gypsum mortar and layers of light earth tiles, covered with stone, which local people were trained to produce and build. Other parts of the complex use local sandstone for traditional dry-stone walls, concrete, timber and recycled materials, aiding low environmental impact: additionally, respect for the sacred nature of the site meant the ground was disturbed as little as possible. Inside, large windows and oculi in the domes provide natural lighting that alters in intensity in the more sacred areas, whereas the shape and materials of the vaults aid natural heat control and acoustics.

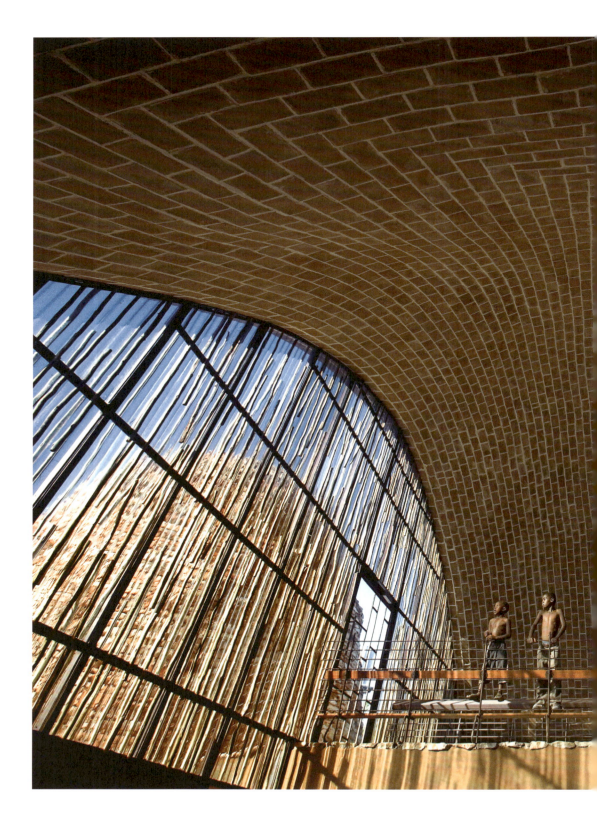

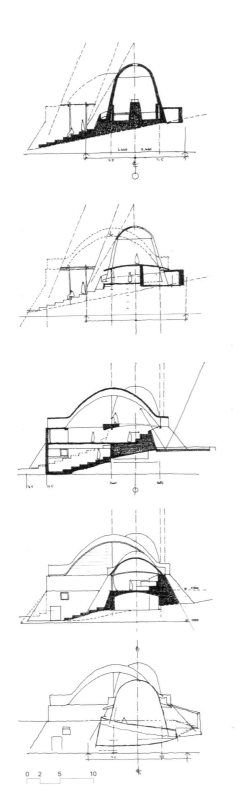

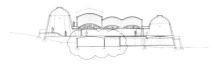

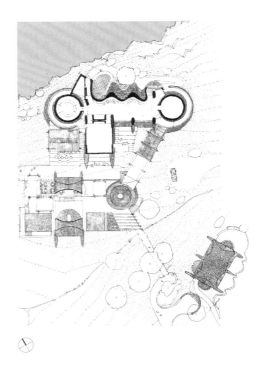

MAPUNGUBWE INTERPRETATION CENTRE
Limpopo Province, South Africa

CLIENT
South African National Parks, Pretoria, South Africa

ARCHITECT
Peter Rich Architects, Johannesburg, South Africa:
Peter Rich, principal
Timothy Hall, project architect

DESIGNER AND STRUCTURAL ENGINEERS, TILE VAULTS
Michael Ramage, University of Cambridge, University Senior Lecturer in Architectural Engineering, fellow and tutor, Sidney Sussex College, Cambridge, UK

John Ochsendorf, MIT, Department of Architecture, associate professor, Boston, USA

STRUCTURAL ENGINEER
Henry Fagan & Partners, Cape Town, South Africa,

VAULT CONSTRUCTION TRAINING AND SUPERVISION
Re-Vault, Whangarei, New Zealand:
James Bellamy, principal

CONTRACTOR
USNA Builders, Louis Trichardt, South Africa

QUANTITY SURVEYOR
DH Construction Techniques, Johannesburg, South Africa

PROJECT DATA
Site area: 2750 m^2
Total built area: 1130 m^2
Cost: 1,875,000 USD
Commission: December 2005
Design: March 2006–August 2007
Construction: October 2007–June 2009
Completion: December 2009

PETER RICH
Peter Rich Architects is a practice dedicated to the creation of authentic and contemporary African architecture.
For over 30 years, Peter Rich has been rigorously engaged in four key areas of architectural practice. As a researcher, he pioneered the documentation of African vernacular architecture researching "Ndebele" settlements. His passion and discoveries have been brought to a worldwide audience through extensive publication and prolific lecturing. In his role as professor at the University of the Witwatersrand, he developed a contemporary architectural vocabulary that built on these traditions and, through teaching, helped to empower successive generations of young architects.
As a practicing architect for over 30 years, he has endeavoured to put his research and ideas into built form, working at a variety of scales – from individual houses through to city master plans. In recognition of his work, Rich was awarded an Honorary Fellowship of the American Institute of Architects in 2009 and a South African Institute of Architects Gold Medal in 2010.
Principal of Peter Rich Architects, based in Johannesburg, South Africa, Rich is also a founding partner of Light Earth Designs, with Timothy Hall and Michael Ramage, a practice based in the UK and Rwanda dedicated to furthering labour-intensive vaulted architecture and sustainable technological solutions in the developing world.

WEBSITES
www.sanparks.org/parks/mapungubwe
www.peterricharchitects.co.za

BUILDING CRAFTS IN THE MODERN WORLD
Omar Abdulaziz Hallaj

The Master Jury of the Aga Khan Award for Architecture took a bold stance to pass on a strong message about the importance of craft in the making of architecture, both as a marker of community identity and as a process of producing excellence in design. At the risk of seeming nostalgic and having a very narrow vision regarding the scope of architectural practices within Muslim communities, the Jury opted for a shortlist and a final selection that brings the role of craftsmanship to the very core of the question of modernity. Modernity has for so long been defined as antithetical to the small-scale production techniques often ascribed to traditional building processes. The Jury's decision is an invitation to revisit the paradigms of authenticity, identity and environmental harmony that so often stereotyped the discussion. By shifting attention to accountability, process and sustainability, we have an altogether new vantage point to evaluate craftsmanship in the built environment.

To reframe the question of craft we need to look beyond the traditional aspect of technique and social meaning. This has evolved through the ages, albeit in small increments, making it rather difficult to see its evolution from one generation to the next, which leads to the misconstrued idea of tradition as something fixed in time. Most of the debate about craft in recent years (perhaps since William Morris) has evolved about its cultural relevance. We had to imbue it with cultural significance and valorise it to exact funding for it to thrive. Most arguments for craft revolve around our way of life, identity, spiritual link to the past, authenticity, naturalism, fear of the modern and so on. In essence, we find justifications for its continued valuation beyond its economic obsolescence, at best as a moral prerogative. To that extent, paying for craftsmanship (a not so rational economic activity in the modern world) has fallen under the categories of luxury, the arts and the cultural; categories that have been reified to justify their keep. The sustainability of funding for craft was thus left at the mercy of excess in society, and as part of the political debate over the allocation of that excess.

Craft has always been part of a complex economic and social environment in constant transformation. The moral value of preserving craft must be placed within that evolving framework if we are to avoid the nostalgic portrayal of craft within the dual paradigm of tangible and intangible heritage. Notions such as "living heritage" are themselves modern constructs and part of the reification tool kit. Preserving craft must look at the whole cycle of supply and demand and the influence exercised by one over the other. Influencing that cycle is beyond the realm of intervention of most practitioners of the built environment: architects, conservationists, restorers and so on. Yet, the economic rationale of preserving craft is now creeping into the discourse (creating jobs, attracting tourists, increasing demand and such like) mostly at the elementary discursive level and rarely in tangible economic terms.

Reviving the idea of craftsmanship as a technique can be a difficult undertaking. There are lost skills, lack of incentives for young apprentices, disappearance of primary materials, not to mention that the process requires huge investments in time and money to jump-start the cycle. But often that is the end of any planned intervention for preserving building crafts. The economic rationale for the survival of craft is often driven by one of two forces. On the one hand, a considerable part of funding for the preservation work comes through the generosity of some donor. The nation state is increasingly behaving like a donor. Supporting the preservation of intangible heritage is framed as part of the national undertaking of creating an imagined community. Intervention takes place on the symbolic level, an investment in nation building, often in one-time disbursements.

On the other hand, the most successful programmes for preserving craft have taken place in underdeveloped economies, often with the informal sector dominating the production and consumption cycle. The demand for traditional building crafts has survived because there is still a critical mass of consumers that cannot afford an alternative. In countries where networks for modern economic activities have not been successfully established, old markets have survived both because they represent the only alternative, and as a sign of resistance to the formal economic sector and the introduction of formalised economic flows and credit-based financial systems. The formal economy engenders fees and taxes, extractions that are not acceptable without the accountability of the state to its constituencies in terms of representation and services.

There are three areas that need to be fully explored to understand how craft can be sustained in the modern world beyond the nostalgia of heritage preservation. First, there is the incessant issue of understanding the value chain within which craft is situated. As the process of producing the built environment increases in complexity (competition, availability of supply, the sheer quantity of demand, its quality, affordability, willingness to pay, environmental costs, market trends, delivery networks and so on), craftsmanship is reduced to a gradually smaller portion of the net final value of the product. Whereas in most pre-mechanised and semi-mechanised processes the value of labour could account for as much as two thirds of the final product, in today's world it can often amount to no more than half of that share for the building crafts and often well below that for other types of crafts.

This sliding of the share of craftsmanship down the value chain was accompanied by an intense competition reducing the net sum of the product itself.

The viability of craft must be foremost contextualised in this regard. When the old master builders regret that their way of life and work is no longer attractive to young people, they are often lamenting their own failure to keep up with the economic reality of their trade. Discussing the survival of crafts with old master builders often inadvertently begins with someone saying: "I don't want my child to be in the trade". This can be understood as a reference to the increasingly poor standing of the building trades in the social ranking, while, quite literally, the master builders were lamenting their reduced fortunes in a world that they can no longer influence. The value chains extend well beyond the local context where the value of craftsmanship was traditionally negotiated. How do you price a square metre of mud plaster, or a wooden ceiling? Funding for the work is now structured in these terms. Funding in the past was structured around the value of work put into the job. It is not just a question of reconciliation between two different measurement systems; the epistemological gap is huge.

Architectural preservation often ignores that whole paradigm. Most successful preservation projects (including award-winning projects) work on the basis of upholding old pricing techniques; the typical dialogue between expert supervisor and craftsman is negotiated on the basis of past practices, available budgets and required quality. Funding is always taken for granted once made available for the job, work ending once funding is finished. Of course the process might have secondary effects (externalities). A good product will encourage future demand; often the assumption is that preserving craft makes it replicable once everyone realises how good it is, and its propagation will happen by osmosis. How often do we hear donors wanting to fund pilot projects, with the underpinning message that a positive practice will be replicated somehow? In more advanced situations we are starting to hear terms such as handover, local ownership, sustainability plan and exit strategy. We are still missing the point. Value chains can only be sustained once they are considered from beginning to end.

To break the demand cycle, the second important aspect of preserving craft is about accountability. In the current thinking about valuing craftsmanship, progressive advances have been made in the production of transferable goods through the fair-trade network. The idea here is to ensure through a revaluation process that a substantial part of the value chain is retained locally by readjusting the production process and ensuring that an increasing part of the value-adding activities are carried by the craftspeople, to increase their share in the final value of the product. The key word in this regard is "fair". How we assess fairness is very much related to how we justify the level of investment we put into the structural readjustment of the production process, but, more importantly, in justifying how we price the product. In most fair-trade situations, we are augmenting the share of the craftspeople in the final product by shifting the burden of the surplus cost to an external market, slightly larger than the local one and capable, because of excess in consumption power, to absorb the additional cost of "fairness" both in financial and moral terms.

In the built environment, that transfer is not as practical. The only way to externalise the cost is often indirectly through tourism, which, to a certain extent, provides a comparable economic process to export and is often classified as an export industry. If properly restructured, revenues from tourism can be structurally readjusted to allow for a "fair" share of national revenues to return to the craftspeople. The building up of the national accountability towards the production of crafts and intangible heritage is a very complex, if not impossible, economic and political process. Even in the most advanced and enlightened economic discourses on heritage preservation, we see a wide gap. National and international donors still fail to understand the valuation of craft as a question of fairness of distribution of burdens and revenues.

The dominant discourse is still defined by the issue of subsidy to the public realm versus subsidy to the private realm. We often ignore that the economies of scale needed to preserve craftsmanship for the public realm are not possible without the same crafts being supported in the private realm. And yet, how do you make the spending on craft in the private realm accountable or even justifiable? Very clearly, the extended value chains needed to sustain crafts can no longer be limited to local contexts. Fairness arguments cannot be limited to the contribution intangible heritage makes to the national tourism bottom line. Even in countries where the state taxation system is quite capable of recuperating the indirect benefits of tourism and of refocusing them to the preservation of the heritage assets (that generated the tax base in the first base), the process is hardly transparent.

In other countries, that rationale is almost impossible to sustain. The state hardly collects taxes and can hardly attribute the taxes it collects to direct or indirect sources. The process of taxation is a complex issue and in many countries it is simply not an economic topic. The whole issue of the accountability of taxation is at the core. Democratisation, social contracts and transparency are hallmarks of the discussion on taxes and fairness in the distribution of state rents. The state is often happy to subsidise some aspects of preservation, albeit at a limited level, to avoid the discussion on accountability of public funds. The preservation of a market place becomes a compromise to avoid the issue related to the reform of the economic performance of the state. The traditional is transformed into a strategy for eluding formalisation. Preserving intangible cultural heritage is subsequently framed as an act of reconciliation between the formal economic power of the state and the informal resistance to that power, a process that is hardly sustainable even if one can celebrate its success in temporarily preserving "heritage".

On the reverse side of the accountability issue is the responsibility of the craftspeople themselves to the final consumers. We fantasise about the old days, where craftspeople used to produce quality work because of ethical norms, mystic devotion and mutual reciprocity. In reality, crafts were always regulated through the guilds, the official controller (the *muhtasib*) and the legal system. Today, in the desperate attempt to preserve the last vestiges of crafts, we tend to exempt them from being accountable to anything but the expert opinion of the conservationist who authorises the payment. By actually removing the crafts products from formal and informal accreditation processes, we are contributing to their devaluation. Part of reinvigorating the value of crafts is to re-immerse them in accreditation systems and not shield them. In the past, craftspeople used their accountability as part of their marketing strategies. Of course traditional crafts will not survive the scrutiny of most modern building standards. Or will they? That is a question that will require considerable discussion. One thing is certain: without accountability, the only value of the crafts will be aesthetic and will endure only as far as demand fancies its relevance.

The last point that needs to be discussed in the context of crafts is whether craft can withstand the need for change and continued relevance? Can it adapt? Can it be innovative? In reality, any acute art or architectural historian will readily jump to provide the answer. What kind of a silly question is that? Crafts have continuously evolved and adapted, have always been innovative, have been influenced by trends and generated innovations in their own rights. The framing of crafts under the rubric of tradition has, by contrast, created a halo of sacredness around these production processes. They justify their keep within the current funding structures by adhering strictly to an imagined and idealised form. Innovation becomes the antithesis of preservation. As heritage is codified for symbolic consumption as a signifier of national unity, innovation becomes synonymous with the fast-changing modern world. "Inspired by tradition" is another compromise that has emerged as part of the reification tool kit. It softens the control on the rigidity of symbolic preservation, albeit still within the framework of mystifying the past as a separate category than the present.

What are the determining factors for ensuring that crafts do not become a mediocre pretext for curbing innovation and adaptability? Most of the projects that were shortlisted and all the projects that were premiated by the Award this cycle have had to respond to this question in one way or another. While asking the deeper questions about process was at the core of the Jury discussion, it is not preservation that dominated the discussion, I believe. But, how do we ensure that form-making is accountable to questions of sustainability, relevance and creativity? In holding onto the crafts as tradition, many parts of the Muslim *umma* are simply avoiding the deeper questions of modernity. How do Muslim communities fit in the modern world, economically, socially and culturally? We have the Jury of this cycle of the Aga Khan Award for Architecture to thank for reopening this question once more. Beyond the classic formula of heritage preservation, the question of craft was brought to the surface in old and new contexts alike. Its economy of scale and accountability to social processes, as well as its ability to compete and continuously adapt and innovate, are at the forefront of a discussion that must be carried to new levels.

CONSERVATION

How do we benefit from and embrace the architectural and physical contributions of our ancestors? Projects such as the Preservation of Sacred and Collective Oasis Sites, Restoration of Thula Fort, Revitalisation of Birzeit Historic Centre and Rehabilitation of Nagaur Fort both celebrate and learn from the achievements of the past. But they also create exemplary evidence of living heritage that once again becomes a part of our contemporary lives and experiences.

PRESERVATION OF SACRED AND COLLECTIVE OASIS SITES
Guelmim Region, Morocco

Since 2003, architect and anthropologist Salima Naji has worked to save the built heritage, but also the cultural and spiritual values and traditions, of the oasis towns of southern Morocco. This ambitious undertaking involves four projects that range in scale from communal granaries to partially abandoned fortified towns located in the Guelmim region in the Anti-Atlas Mountains.

This is an extremely arid desert region famous for prehistoric petroglyphs. The existence of underground aquifers and dry river beds (*wadi*) that flood during the rainy season led to a sophisticated management of scarce water resources and man-made oases that allow for sustainable agriculture. Naturally, towns developed around these verdant depressions, linked by caravan routes across the Sahara and West Africa to the Atlantic and Mediterranean. Grain was held to be sacred and the Berbers' collective grain stores were consequently also holy sites, even after their conversion to Islam, and many include mosques and tombs in or near them.

Today, the old mud towns are often abandoned and the granaries in decay, despite their importance for communal identity, while traditional building skills have been lost as the trend for a standardised architecture of breeze blocks and concrete steadily creeps in from the north to fashion the new towns, with modern amenities, that spring up alongside the old.

Naji aims to rectify this by restoring awareness and a sense of "ownership" in local communities for their historic monuments and public spaces, engaging new and traditional community groups in a participatory process that will ultimately benefit local use and local purposes, training and employing local workers, and, in the long term, promoting earthen architecture as sustainable and affordable for contemporary living.

For example, in the 13th-century fortified town of Assa, the earthen ramparts, towers and gates were restored; streets and public spaces (now used for festivals and weddings) were improved; the religious schools and mosques were rehabilitated (and now much reused by locals); and several private houses were also renovated that will have a "public" use as restaurants and guest houses, attracting tourism (while the families have often returned to live in them during the hottest months). Instead, at Amtoudi, two granaries were stabilised and partially reconstructed and the community hopes to incorporate them into tourist circuits. These projects provide an alternative model for the conservation of old towns and historic monuments in Morocco.

PRESERVATION OF SACRED AND COLLECTIVE OASIS SITES
Guelmim Region, Morocco

CLIENTS
Agence pour le Développement des Provinces du Sud, Rabat, Morocco:
Hajji Ahmed, general director
Rah Lahoucine, regional director

Cooperazione Internazionale Sud Sud, Palermo, Italy:
Massimiliano Di Tota, coordinator Morocco (2009–10)
Elmar Loreti, coordinator Morocco (2011–13)
Calogero Messina, project local manager (2009–10)
Giovanna Dibenedetto, project local manager (2010–12)

Local Communities:
Assa's traditional local council:
Ahchouch Houssein Afqir, Tayeb Lassaoui, Waissi Hamdi
Amtoudi's municipal council:
Aguinou Lahoucine, president of the local association
Amtoudi's traditional local council:
Haj Aguinou Abdellah, Achik Abdellah, Abderahman Driouch, Aderdor Lahcen
Agadir Ouzrou's traditional local council:
El Harwi Lhoucine, Jaafari Mohammed, Lahcen Ouchoua, community officer

ARCHITECT
Salima Naji, Kenitra, Morocco

DEVELOPMENT EXPERT
David Goeury, Laboratoire Espace Nature et Culture, Paris IV-La Sorbonne, Paris, France

CONTRACTOR
Socorouissi, Laayoune, Morocco:
Hassane Jerrar, CEO

MASTER BUILDERS
Amtoudi Master Builders:
Haj Aguinou Abdellah, Achik Abdellah, Abderahman Driouch, Aderdor Lahcen

Assa Master Builders:
Ba Moh Lahcen, Chajii Brahim, El Qabab Mohamed, Outzoumert Mahmoud

Agadir Ouzrou Master Builders:
Bilal Ettaqi, Mbark Bousgane, Ali Messaoudi, Abdellah Boulman

PROJECT DATA
Amtoudi granaries
Site area: 4276 m^2
Cost: 69,000 USD
Commission: February 2007
Design: January 2003–April 2006
Construction: July 2007–January 2008
Completion: January 2008

Ksar Assa
Site area: 25,197 m^2
Cost: 1,620,000 USD
Commission: December 2005
Design: January 2006–March 2010
Construction: February 2006–November 2011
Completion: June 2007–November 2011

Ksar Agadir Ouzrou
Site area: 1800 m^2
Cost: 49,000 USD
Commission: January 2008
Design: March 2008–December 2008
Construction: May 2009–October 2011
Completion: October 2009–October 2011

AGENCE POUR LE DÉVELOPPEMENT DES PROVINCES DU SUD
The Agency for Promotion and Economic and Social Development of the Southern Provinces of the Kingdom, which embraces an area covering 60% of Moroccan territory and includes more than a million inhabitants, has been established to develop the infrastructure of the region, and to implement different territorial and sectorial programmes. It aims to provide both jobs and income-generating activities, based on the enhancement of local resources.

SALIMA NAJI
Salima Naji completed her architectural studies at the Paris-La Villette School of Architecture and her PhD in Anthropology at the School for Advanced Studies in Social Sciences (Paris). She has studied traditional architecture in southern Morocco for 20 years and has published six books. She created her own agency in 2004 and specialises in sustainable and participative development.

WEBSITES
www.lagencedusud.gov.ma
www.salimanaji.org

RESTORATION OF THULA FORT
Thula, Yemen

Perched on top of a dramatic rocky outcrop, the earliest remains of Thula Fort date back 3000 years. It stands high above the well-preserved walled historic town of Thula, clinging vertically to the steep slopes below, some 50 kilometres from the capital Sana'a. Thula was probably a Sabaean religious site for the worship of a water god, since its location near the Western Highlands guarantees a certain amount of rain per year. This, coupled with the site's defensive value, led to the development of the Fort and fortified town around the natural rainwater channels that were subsequently incorporated into cisterns and an intricate system of waterworks leading down the hillside to the town and its agricultural land, which permitted its occupation for thousands of years.

A new road to Thula in the 1990s opened up the isolated town but brought with it unplanned urban development that started to compromise the architectural and historic integrity of the Fort. Alarmed, the town council sought funding to undertake restoration work. A detailed needs assessment was carried out and, after the discovery of a significant Sabaean-period monumental gateway (1st century BC) among other things, the project broadened in scope to become a multi-phase joint conservation-archaeology initiative.

The walls and gates of the town – typifying Yemeni architecture and characterised by multi-storey residential units built of local stone – were restored first, together with the winding trails and steep steps leading up to the Fort, which covers an area of 8754 square metres, mainly of walled open areas. Inside the Fort, missing parts were integrated and sensitive restoration was carried out on its curtain walls, towers and gates, the stepped paths leading up to the higher levels, the agricultural terraces within its walls, and its elaborate rainwater collection system of channels and pools, the latter especially benefiting local households and agriculture. Traditional materials – stone, wood, mud plaster – were salvaged or sourced locally, technology specific to the region was employed and almost all the labour force came from Thula old town.

The Fort, with its stunning views, is now a popular visitor attraction – for locals and foreigners alike. Future plans include ongoing conservation around the Fort, providing interpretation of it, and further developing it as a tourist/leisure venue.

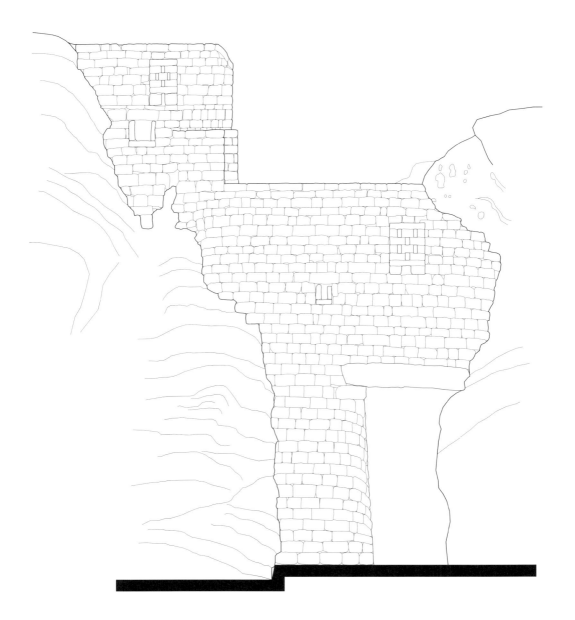

RESTORATION OF THULA FORT
Thula, Yemen

CLIENTS
Social Fund for Development, Sana'a, Yemen:
Abdul Kareem al-Arhabi, former executive director
Abdullah al-Dailami, head of Cultural Heritage Unit
Hafaz al-Dhrahani, head of Amran Branch
Ali Al-Kamli, project officer, Amran Branch

Thula Local Council, Yemen:
Foaid al-Ansi, director of Thula district
Adel al-Najar, president of the local council
Abdul Kareem al-Akawa, coordinator and project director
Khalid al-Zuhari, director of the Fort area

ARCHITECT
Abdullah al-Hadhrami, Sana'a, Yemen

SITE TEAM
Old Town of Thula, Amran Governorate, Yemen:
Harbia al-Himiary, civil engineer
Hamid al-Boni, contractor
Mohamed al-Hakeemi, former site supervisor
Waleed al-Selwi, accountant for the project
Mohamed Ghlab, assistant site supervisor
Abdul Hakim Othman, former site supervisor
Muneeb al-Rajehi, site supervisor
Basam Qadri, accountant
Adel Mansar, assistant site supervisor

CONSULTANT
Al-Jolahi for Consulting, Sana'a, Yemen

ARCHAEOLOGICAL TEAMS
University of Sana'a, Yemen:
Abdo Othman, scientific supervisor
Mohamed al-Haj, archaeologist and field supervisor

General Organisation of Antiquities, Museums and Manuscripts, Sana'a, Yemen:
Khalid Al-Haj, archaeologist and field supervisor
Abdullah Ishaq, archaeologist
Azziz al-Ghori, archaeologist
Saleh Mohsen Mohamed, excavation technician
Abdo Qaid al-Beel, excavation technician
Salah al-Mansuri, archaeologist
Saleh Awdeen, excavation technician

Old Town of Thula, Amran Governorate, Yemen:
Mahr Al-Wajeeh, archaeologist
Ali Mohamed al-Sediq, trainer and excavation technician
Ghanm Mohamed Rafee, trainer and excavation technician
Abdul Nasar al-Shighmimi, architect, documentation specialist
Amin Mihlaj, trainee archaeologist

MASTER MASONS
Old Town of Thula, Amran Governorate, Yemen:
Ali Abo Sied, Mohamed al-Ansi, Mohamed Hani, Ibrahim al-Sheemi, Ali al-Shieb, Hadi al-Qata', master masons
Ali Qasam al-Azaba, mason
Mohamed Ali Abdo, agricultural terraces
Nabil al-Habib, Ali Ahamed al-Madhub, Khalid al-Qata trainers, assistant builder
Ahamed al-Arasi, Ahamed Ateeq, Abdo Sa'ad, Adel al-Arj, Ahmed Salamah, Yahy Dahabah, Yahay Omadi, lime masons
Marzuq Dahabah, Hamid al-Ghobari, Ibrahim al-Ghobari, Mutahar Madhub, stone mason works
Saleh Hani, mud plastering
Hussein al-Nomeili, Mohamed al-Nomeili, rock cutting
Ahmed al-Tawil, carpenter
Araf al-Sanaw, Ali al-Maqahafieh, electricity and sanitation
Sami al-Zalb, guard

PROJECT DATA
Site area: 8754 m^2
Cost: 620,000 USD
Commission: February 2003
Design: March 2004–December 2004
Construction: October 2005–February 2011
Completion: February 2011

ABDULLAH AL-HADHRAMI
Abdullah al-Hadhrami is a Yemeni architect specialised in the conservation and reuse of historic buildings, with extensive experience in the management and coordination of international donors' projects. He has worked as an architect for the private sector, for government agencies and for the Social Fund for Development and Cultural Heritage Protection, with particular reference to interventions in three World Heritage listed sites. He has participated in a number of international conservation and archaeology workshops and was a visiting scholar at the Aga Khan Program for Islamic Architecture at MIT. He has also acted as a cultural heritage expert with UNESCO and the World Bank.

REVITALISATION OF BIRZEIT HISTORIC CENTRE
Birzeit, Palestine

The Palestinian town of Birzeit in the central West Bank is located 11 kilometres north of Ramallah and 25 kilometres north of Jerusalem. Its historic centre covers about four hectares, extending approximately 290 metres from east to west. The town stands at 780 metres above sea level and is surrounded by hills, predominantly terraced for agricultural use and, in particular, for olive groves. In fact, the name of the town reflects the historical importance of olive cultivation and pressing since *bir zeit* refers to the olive-oil storage tanks dug into the ground, several of which are still in existence (although not in use). Birzeit dates back at least to the Byzantine era and seems to have been continuously inhabited. Several archaeological sites, dating to the Byzantine and Roman eras, have been excavated around the perimeter of the town, and many strata exist below the historic centre.

Economic, political and demographic transformations of early- to mid-20th-century Palestine had profound effects on Birzeit, with many residents joining the great waves of Levantine emigration, a process accelerated by international and local events: the world wars, the creation of Israel in 1948, and the Israeli occupation of the West Bank, of the Jordan River and East Jerusalem in 1967. Traditional homes in the historic centre were left to crumble and decay as residents emigrated abroad or built new houses outside the old centre in less congested areas, more conducive to modern lifestyles, being provided with amenities and services lacking in the old town. The Israeli occupation curbed economic development, causing businesses to move out, and streets and public spaces were neglected. This situation was exacerbated in the early 1980s when the dynamic Birzeit University relocated to a site several kilometres to the south, draining a major source of life from the town, although churches and mosques continued to operate.

The 1993 Oslo Accords had profound impacts on Palestinian geography, society and economy, as well as on the built fabric, dramatically reducing the amount of land under Palestinian control and dividing land on the West Bank into areas A (urban, under Palestinian civil and military authority), B (most towns and villages, including Birzeit, under Palestinian civil authority) and C (controlled by Israel, constituting about 60% of land in the West Bank, where the majority of vacant land is located).

Riwaq, a highly respected Palestinian NGO, is one of the key actors lobbying for the protection of the cultural heritage of Palestine. Since its establishment in 1991, it has pursued a multi-tiered strategy that includes documentation, conservation, revitalisation, community participation and activism, legislative reform and lobbying, publicity, job training and public awareness programmes. Since 2007, the cornerstone and guiding strategy of its activities has been the "50 Villages" programme – an ambitious plan to save select villages where an estimated 50% of the surviving historic structures of Palestine are located: part of the group's wide-ranging vision for a continuous Palestinian cultural landscape, against the fragmentation of the post-Oslo period. The vast majority of Palestinians live in the rural B areas, under very difficult economic circumstances. By focusing on villages, Riwaq realised that it could save much of Palestine's remaining heritage, and at the same time have the greatest socio-economic impact. Conservation would create jobs, revitalise local workshops and, ultimately, spark interest and investment in historic village centres. The historic centre of Birzeit, largely intact though much degraded, was the pilot project for the "50 Villages" programme.

Community participation and focus groups were encouraged from the beginning, with local NGOs, residents and other local stakeholders working alongside an active municipality to draft a rehabilitation plan and identify individual projects. When work began in 2008, the population of the old town counted just 183 individuals, representing 36 families. Of these, 16 families owned their premises, and 20 rented. Three businesses were still located there: a mechanic's shop, a grocery store and a bakery. Like other West Bank towns, traditional architecture in the old centre is one-storey high and made of local limestone and lime mortar; houses are one or more square modules, each covered by a dome (*qubba*), and used collectively by the extended family, with concrete, flat-roofed kitchens and bathrooms generally added to the rear.

Riwaq pursued a policy of preventive conservation to upgrade the public realm and restore select public/community buildings to accepted international standards, coupled with creative adaption to embrace modern needs or where the "old" was missing or not restorable, while preserving architectural coherence throughout. Job creation and the revival of affordable traditional techniques and local materials drove the conservation effort, so boosting economic regeneration. Five years of work yielded impressive results: streets have been paved, named and clearly signed; infrastructure upgraded (water) and added to (pipes laid for a future sewer system); facades have been conserved; public spaces have been created (playground) and rehabilitated (courtyards, gardens); and numerous historic buildings have been restored for a variety of uses (community cultural institutions, university residences, tourist accommodation, private businesses…), creating an active cultural hub that is once again coming to life. Cultural heritage conservation is increasingly seen as an important way to preserve collective memory of a historical Palestine for future generations. The successful social, cultural and economic revitalisation of Birzeit undoubtedly stands as an inspiring model for the other villages and rural areas in the "50 Villages" programme and beyond.

JURY CITATION

The Revitalisation of Birzeit Historic Centre is a dynamic project in which the NGO of Riwaq succeeds in mobilising stakeholders and local craftsmen into a process of healing that is not merely physical but that is social, economic and political. By reversing a process of neglect and erasure within a complex and difficult political context, the project manages to transform not only a neglected historic core but also people's lives, and restores not only buildings but the dignity of their users. The project offers an alternative to "museified" historic cores and it pioneers the regeneration of Birzeit's historic centre into cultural infrastructure. It facilitates the reclamation of heritage by the people involved while also allowing them to achieve their self-expressed aspirations. The project is an exemplary dedication to rural heritage that can serve as a model for the 50 villages in which Riwaq is involved, particularly the strategic interventions designed to stimulate long-term development.

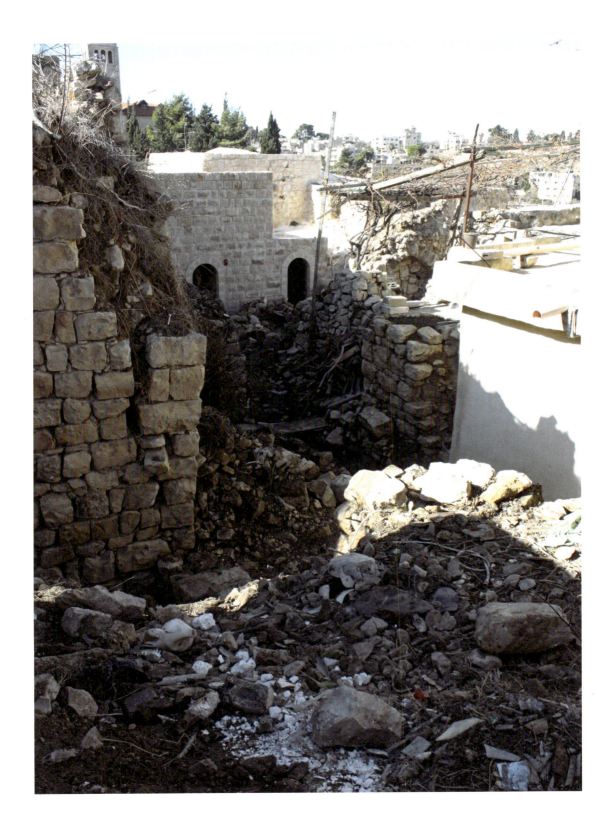

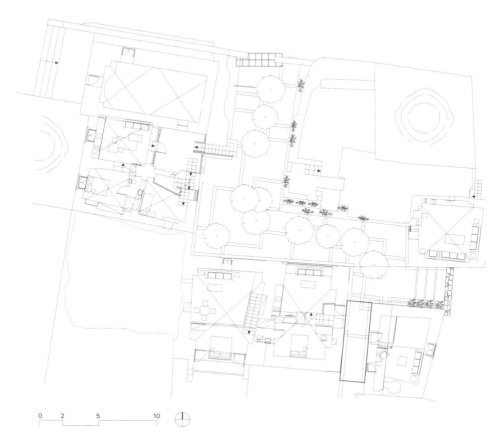

REVITALISATION OF BIRZEIT HISTORIC CENTRE
Birzeit, Palestine

CLIENT
Birzeit Municipality, Palestine:
Yousef Nasser, former mayor
Hasib Al Keileh, mayor
Musa Al Hajj, former director

ARCHITECTS
Riwaq – Centre for Architectural Conservation, Ramallah, Palestine:
Khaldun Bshara, Fida Touma, co-directors
Suad Amiry, founder and former co-director
Nazmi al Jubeh, former co-director
Farhat Muhawi, Birzeit project director
Iyad Issa, Shata Safi, architect planners
Ruba Saleem, Ghada Mubarak, Bilal Abu Faza'a, Khalil Rabah, Lana Judeh, Sahar Qawasmi, Michel Salameh, Renad Shqeirat, Yousef Taha, architects
Tariq Dar Nasser, Nizam 'Owaidat, civil engineers

Rozana Association, Birzeit, Palestine:
Raed Sa'adeh, director

Ministry of Local Government, Ramallah, Palestine:
Shuruq Jaber, architect

Birzeit Municipality, Palestine:
Noor Khdairi, Rana Shaka'a, architects

CONSULTANTS
Birzeit University, Palestine:
Yazid Anani, assistant professor
Samir Baidoon, chair of Business Administration College
In'am Obeidi, Media Studies Programme faculty member
Luna Shamieh, assistant to the dean of Public Policy and Administration College
Nazmi Jubeh, professor

Golzari NG Architects, London, UK:
Nasser Golzari, founder and partner
Yara Sharif, partner

Ministry of Justice, Ramallah, Palestine:
Walid Badawi, director

Solution for Development Consulting, Ramallah, Palestine:
Joudeh Iyad, director

In'ash Al Usra Society, al Bireh, Palestine:
Najla Barakat, assistant director of community research

Dar Al-Tifel Al-Arabi Organisation, Jerusalem:
Baha Jubeh, curator of Palestine Heritage Museum

Friends Schools in Ramallah, Palestine:
Farhat Muhawi, chief architect/planner

Palestine Investment Fund, al Bireh, Palestine:
Maher Saleh Hamayel, CRS supervisor

FUNDING
Swedish International Development Agency, Stockholm, Sweden

Birzeit Pharmaceutical Company, Birzeit, Palestine

Institut du Patrimoine Wallon, Namur, Belgium

Representative Office of the Kingdom of the Netherlands in Ramallah, Palestine

PROJECT DATA
Site area: 40,640 m^2
Cost: 1,458,000 USD
Commission: June 2006
Design: January 2007–November 2011
Construction: January 2008–January 2012
Occupancy: January 2009–ongoing

RIWAQ
Riwaq is a non-governmental, non-profit organisation established in 1991. Riwaq's main aim is the documentation, rehabilitation and development of the architectural heritage of Palestine. This signifies the protection of *all* layers, styles and remains of all periods and civilisations that once existed in Palestine. The various strata tell us the story of the rich, varied and complex identity of Palestine; they also negate the "purity" of the politically charged one-layer identity. This approach signifies the protection of not only noble architectural and religious sites, but also the valuable and varied urban, peasant and nomad architecture. The main objective, challenge and dream of Riwaq, at this point, is to convince the public at large, and decision makers in particular, that historic buildings and historic centres can and should be seen as an important tool for socio-economic-political development rather than as a liability.

WEBSITE
www.riwaq.org

REHABILITATION OF NAGAUR FORT
Nagaur, Rajasthan, India

The ancient city of Nagaur in central Rajasthan was one of the first strongholds of Muslim power (12th–16th century) in northern India. Located on a major caravan route, it was also an important centre of Sufism, learning and pilgrimage. Nagaur Fort sits on a small hill and occupies an area of approximately 15 hectares, encircled by the historic town with its two- to three-storey-high, flat-roof houses and narrow meandering streets. Built in the 12th century and repeatedly added to and altered over subsequent centuries, the Fort comprises 60 low-rise buildings and five palaces, with open space and landscaped gardens, all enclosed by 1.8 kilometres of perimeter walls. It is a fine blend of Rajput and Mughal architecture that had fallen into disrepair.

The rehabilitation project sought principally to restore and bring back to life the entire Fort complex, to increase public awareness of its heritage value and to make it fully accessible to and usable by the public – both local and foreign. Guided by the principles of minimum intervention and through the use of traditional methods and materials – stone, lime and wood – in its restoration, the project also aimed to re-establish vernacular skills and create new opportunities and livelihoods for the local people.

In 1993 a Conservation Master Plan was drafted and all buildings and grounds were documented and assessed for adaptive reuse. Initial conservation concentrated on arresting further damage: walls, roofs and foundations were stabilised and repaired; important wall paintings were discovered and saved; open spaces were cleared. The intricate water system – an underlying concept behind the original planning of the whole Fort complex, serving to collect and channel precious rainwater in an arid climate – was discovered and restored and today seven water bodies, four wells, one step well and a hundred fountains are fully functioning. The historic entry system of a barbican and six successive gateways was also reclaimed. Reuse work progressed at the same time: the Queens' Palaces were converted into hotel suites and a well-planned visitor route was established for guided tours around what is now a palace site-cum-museum. The local community can enjoy the lush replanted gardens and local worshippers now have easy access to repaired temples.

Today, the Fort is a venue for cultural, social and religious activities, among which the Sufi Music Festival, and its ongoing conservation means that it has become a laboratory for experts, scholars and students.

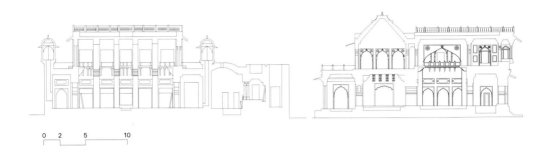

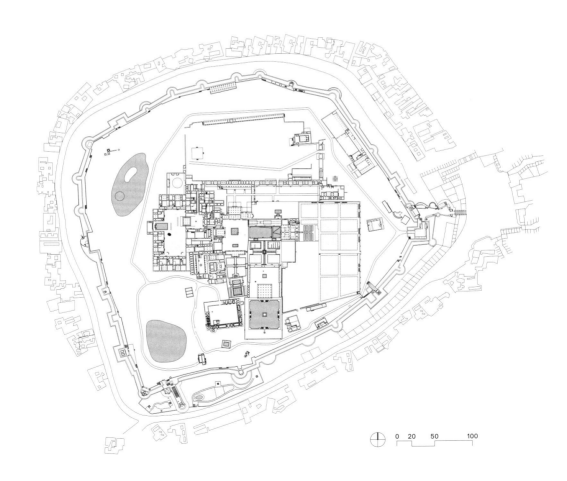

REHABILITATION OF NAGAUR FORT
Nagaur, Rajasthan, India

CLIENT
Mehrangarh Museum Trust, Jodhpur, Rajasthan, India:
His Highness Maharaja Gaj Singh II, managing trustee
Her Highness Maharani Hemlata Rajye,
Baijilal Shivranjani Rajye, Yuvraj Shivraj Singh,
R. K. Martand Singh, Th. Jaswant Singh Jasol,
O. P. Agarwal, Shobita Punja, Mahrukh Tarapor, trustees
Karni Jasol, director of Mehrangarh Museum Trust
Mahendra Singh, former chief executive officer
Shailesh Mathur, engineering manager
Shiv Singh, supervisor
Surendra Harsh, site engineer

ARCHITECT
Minakshi Jain Architect, Ahmedabad, India:
Minakshi Jain, principal
Kulbhushan Jain, architect planner
Sunil Prajapati, draftsman
Jitendra Sharma, Poonam Jolly, junior architects

CONTRACTORS
Gokal Ram Makad, Arjun Prajapati, Ashok Makad, Jodhpur, India

Dilawar Khan, Emamuddin, Ghevwar Chand, Jagdish Prasad, Mool Chand, Poonam Chand, Safi Khan, Nagaur, India

MASTER CRAFTSMEN
Sukha Ram, Faizu Khan, Nagaur, India

WATER SUPPLY AND SANITATION CONSULTANT
Jay Consultant, Ahmedabad, India:
Arwin Mewada

TEXTILE CONSULTANT
M/S Gitto, Jaipur, India:
Madhurima Patni, Brigitte Singh

LANDSCAPE CONSULTANTS
School of Planning and Architecture, New Delhi:
Priyaleen Singh

Pradip Krishen, New Delhi, India

ELECTRICAL CONSULTANT
Harshad B Jhaveri and Jhaveri Associates, Ahmedabad, India:
Harshad Jhaveri

FOUNTAIN CONSULTANT
J. K. Agri Corporation, Ahmedabad, India:
K. K. Patel

PROJECT DATA
Site area: 145,686 m^2
Length of perimeter walls: 1.8 km
Cost: 1,970,000 USD
Commission: January 1993
Construction: April 1993–November 2008
Design: January 1993–April 2005
Completion: April 2002–November 2008

MEHRANGARH MUSEUM TRUST
Mehrangarh Museum Trust is a leading cultural institution established in 1972 by the 36th Custodian of Marwar-Jodhpur, His Highness Maharaja Gaj Singh II, and has a unique importance as a repository of the artistic and cultural history of a large area of Rajasthan, Marwar-Jodhpur. The Trust has dedicated itself to the preservation and development of the rich tangible and intangible heritage of Marwar. It has participated in many international exhibitions and invited scholars of different fields to research the heritage of Marwar. The Trust has received the UNESCO Asia-Pacific "Award of Excellence" in the field of Architectural Conservation, Cultural Heritage and Adaptive Reuse in 2002 and 2005, and the Fassa Bortolo Domus Award for Architectural Conservation in 2012.

MINAKSHI JAIN
Minakshi Jain is recognised as a leading authority on architectural conservation in India and has been involved in teaching and practice for over 35 years.
After graduating from architectural school, Minakshi worked with Charles and Ray Eames on their project "My India My People" at the National Institute of Design, Ahmedabad. She then studied under Louis Kahn in the 1960s, and returned to India to set up an architectural practice with her husband Kulbhushan Jain. Apart from her practice, Minakshi has been teaching for the last 30 years as a visiting faculty member at the Centre for Environmental Planning and Technology (CEPT), and she has co-authored and published several books on Indian architecture.
She has received many awards, including a scholarship for flying single-engine aircraft back in the 1960s to the more recent UNESCO Award of Excellence in Conservation.

WEBSITES
www.mehrangarh.org
www.worldsufispiritfestival.org/nagaur-venues.php

DWELLING

Residential projects provide the basic need for the intimacy of shelter. Projects such as Apartment No. 1 and the Met Tower provide alternative approaches to how the theme of dwelling can be revisited. Whether through the consideration of opportunities offered by the choice of a material and its subsequent impact on design and construction or through climate and density, these projects highlight the importance of the need for the constant re-evaluation of housing and of the spaces of domesticity.

APARTMENT NO. 1
Mahallat, Iran

Located at a relatively high altitude on a flattish plain, Mahallat is an ancient town in Markazi province in central Iran that has benefited over the centuries from an abundance of thermal springs and surrounding mountains boasting a multitude of stone deposits. Today, the latter accounts for more than 50% of the local economy in the form of stonecutting factories and stone export. However, more than 50% of the stones worked, totalling some 365,000 tons per year, are discarded during the process.

The project aimed to redress this situation and successfully demonstrated – locally and abroad – that the recycling of discarded stone is not only cost-effective, energy-saving and environmentally friendly but can also be aesthetically pleasing and innovative.

The five-storey mixed-use building, comprising two ground-floor retail spaces and eight three-bedroom apartments above, stands slightly higher than the city centre and is visible from afar. It presents innovative facades of recycled stones, which are very durable, need little maintenance, facilitate insulation and temperature control, protect the building against rain and allow it to breathe. The pierced perimeter walls of the communal courtyard and some freestanding interior walls are also made of these discarded stones, which are variable in shape, size and colour but have a distinctive uniform thickness. The addition of triangular stone protrusions on the two shorter fronts ingeniously creates rectangular rooms inside the apartments, overcoming the restrictions of the irregular shape of the lot, and at the same time sheltering smaller windows below them and animating the facades. Larger windows have wooden shutters, inspired by old Mahallati doors, that fold back along rails and allow residents to control light, temperature and privacy levels and that are also a distinctive feature of the exterior.

The interiors feature distinct private and public areas, while communal space is provided in the minimally landscaped courtyard and panoramic rooftop area.

Emulating strong sharp forms found in the quarries nearby, the austere presence of the building – enlivened by the play between abstract volumes and massing, shadows and voids, textures and colours, contemporary design and traditional concepts – has already become an icon in the town and a model for new directions in contemporary building design.

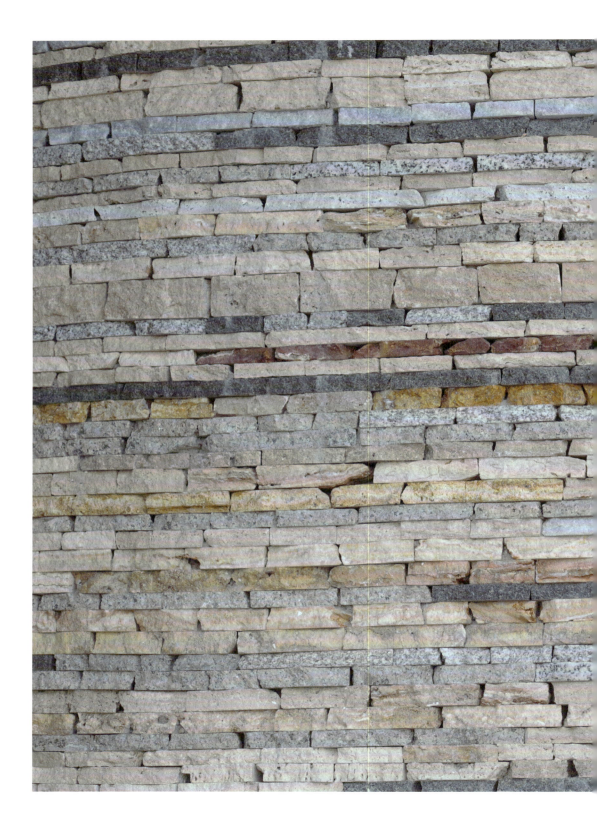

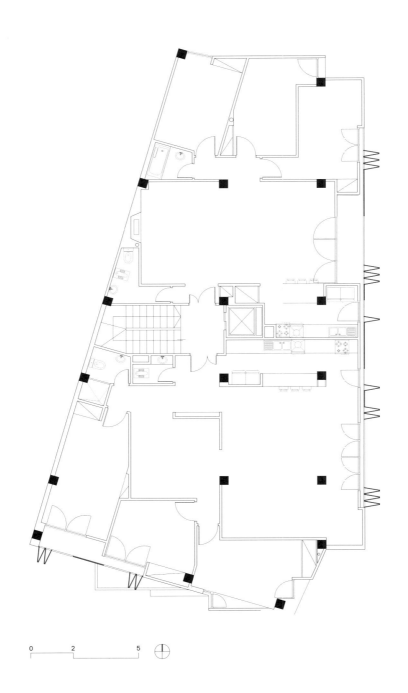

APARTMENT NO. 1
Mahallat, Iran

CLIENTS
Ramin Mehdizadeh, Hossein Sohrabpoor, Mehdi Mehdizadeh, Tehran, Iran

ARCHITECT
AbCT – Architecture by Collective Terrain, Tehran, Iran/Washington DC, USA: Ramin Mehdizadeh, founder and architect

CONTRACTOR
Mehdi Mehdizadeh, Tehran, Iran

STRUCTURAL ENGINEER
Reza Mehdizadeh, Tehran, Iran

MECHANICAL ENGINEER
Ehsan Mehdizadeh, Tehran, Iran

PROJECT DATA
Site area: 420 m^2
Ground-floor area: 260 m^2
Cost: 660,000 USD
Commission: August 2007
Design: August 2007–December 2007
Construction: January 2008–August 2010
Completion: September 2010

RAMIN MEHDIZADEH
Born in Ahwaz, Iran, in 1976, architect Ramin Mehdizadeh gained his Master's Degrees in Architecture at the National University of Iran, Tehran, and in Real Estate Development at Columbia University in New York.
During his time with Skidmore, Owings & Merrill, New York, in 2007–08, his projects included the schematic design drawings, the design development drawings and the construction document drawing sets for Moynihan Station Redevelopment (Penn Station), New York, for Madison Square Garden, and also for the National University of Singapore in 2008 and for Mumbai International Airport, India, the same year. From 2009, with his partners, he founded Architecture by Collective Terrain (AbCT), a full-service international architectural firm based in Tehran, Seoul and Washington DC, specialised in projects in Asia and the Middle East. The design of Apartment No. 1 in Mahallat gained Mehdizadeh first place in the Grand Me'mar Award, 2010. This project has been published in many international architectural magazines, such as *Architectural Design*, *The Plan* and *Atlas: Architectures of the 21st Century – Africa and Middle East 2012*, and is illustrated on many architectural websites. Mehdizadeh was also awarded the World Architecture Community Award, New York, 2008, and the plaque of the first ranked Architect of the Year, 2010, Tehran, Iran.

WEBSITE
www.abct.kr

THE MET TOWER
Bangkok, Thailand

The Met is a 66-storey, 230-metre-tall residential high-rise in central Bangkok, a city that has one of the fastest rates in the world for erecting high-rise buildings. Almost none of these are designed for natural ventilation and most are sealed, glazed, curtain-wall towers emulating cold-climate models, with little differentiation between commercial or residential typologies and no interchange between outside and in.

The design of the Met, instead, aimed to address the issue of high-rise, high-density living in the tropics, where there is year-round light wind, constant warm temperatures and high humidity, by adapting the local vernacular and passive strategies of traditional low-rise timber houses for living in the sky. The skyscraper is comprised of 370 stacked apartments of 2, 3, 4 bedrooms and penthouse layout types in three main towers or six interconnected smaller towers arranged in a staggered block configuration on top of a 9-storey car-parking podium. The towers can "breathe" as the core has been "pulled apart" to establish a one-apartment-deep solution so that light and air reach every side. The core is a series of vast vertical voids that occupy the full height of the building and transform the spaces in between the staggered towers into breezeways: consequently wind swirls through the structure, natural ventilation is constant, each of the blocks is shaded by the other and there is no need for air conditioning.

Sky bridges accommodating private terraces, outdoor living areas, high-rise gardens and pools, and a communal 50-metre-long swimming pool, library, gym, spa and other facilities link the towers horizontally every six storeys and act as structural bracing. Vertically, the reinforced-concrete columns are set on a 4.5-metre grid, making up 9-metre-wide modules that are appropriate for all the various functions – apartments, recreational facilities and car parking. The columns extend on the exterior providing shade and creating protected indoor-outdoor spaces for balconies and terraces, emphasising the slender massing of the structure, especially when lit up at night.

Contemporary interpretations of traditional Thai elements on the facades also relate the building to the city and its context: for example, randomly placed mirrored stainless-steel pleated panels recall the sparkling mirrors of Thai temples; cladding recalls Thai temple tiles; and the staggered balconies recall traditional timber panelling on Thai houses or Thai textiles. The Met is already a trendsetter in high-rise residential development in Thailand and South-East Asia as a whole.

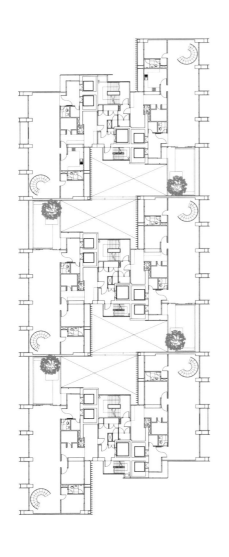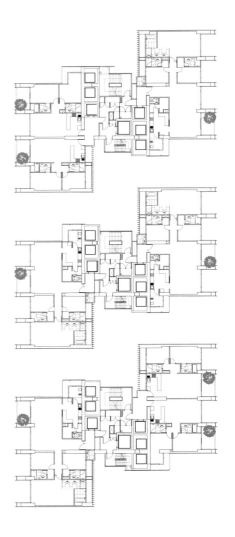

THE MET TOWER
Bangkok, Thailand

CLIENT
Pebble Bay Thailand Company, Bangkok, Thailand

ARCHITECT
WOHA Architects, Singapore:
Wong Mun Summ, Richard Hassell, founding directors
Sim Choon Heok, Punpong Wiwatkul, Puiphai Khunawat, Alina Yeo, Techit Romraruk, Jose Nixon Sicat, Cheah Boon Kwan, Carina Tang, Gerry Richardson, Janita Han, project team

ASSOCIATED ARCHITECT
Tandem Architects 2001, Bangkok, Thailand

STRUCTURAL ENGINEER
Worley Parsons, Bangkok, Thailand

MECHANICAL AND ELECTRICAL ENGINEER
Lincolne Scott Ng, Singapore

QUANTITY SURVEYOR
KPK Quantity Surveyors, Singapore

LANDSCAPE ARCHITECT
Cicada, Singapore

ENVIRONMENTAL IMPACT ASSESSMENT CONSULTANT
ERM, Siam, Bangkok, Thailand

CONTRACTOR
Bouygues Thai, Bangkok, Thailand

PROJECT DATA
Site area: 11,361 m^2
Total combined floor area: 124,885 m^2
Cost: 132,000,000 USD
Commission: August 2003
Design: March 2004
Construction: August 2005
Completion: December 2009

WOHA
The architecture of WOHA, founded by Wong Mun Summ and Richard Hassell in 1994, is notable for its constant evolution and innovation. A profound awareness of local context and tradition is intertwined with an ongoing exploration of contemporary architectural form-making, sustainable ideas and urban typologies for the tropics, thus creating a unique fusion of practicality and invention. WOHA has won an unprecedented amount of architectural awards for a South-East Asian practice, such as the 2010 International Highrise Award and the 2011 RIBA Lubetkin Prize. In 2007, it received the Aga Khan Award for Architecture for the Moulmein Rise Residential Building. The practice currently has projects under construction in Singapore, India, China, Thailand and Indonesia. A travelling exhibition, entitled "Breathing Architecture", devoted exclusively to their work, opened at the Deutsches Architekturmuseum, Germany, in December 2011, and two substantial monographs – *WOHA: The Architecture of WOHA* and *WOHA: Selected Projects Vol. 1* – have already been published.

WEBSITE
www.woha.net

INFRASTRUCTURE

How do specific artefacts and physical structures facilitate connections and support the operations of a city and of a society? Projects such as the Rehabilitation of Tabriz Bazaar, Rabat-Salé Urban Infrastructure Project, Islamic Cemetery and Salam Centre for Cardiac Surgery are all examples of buildings and structures constructed for the benefit of the public and the better functioning of our civil society. In that sense there are always correlations between infrastructure and democracy.

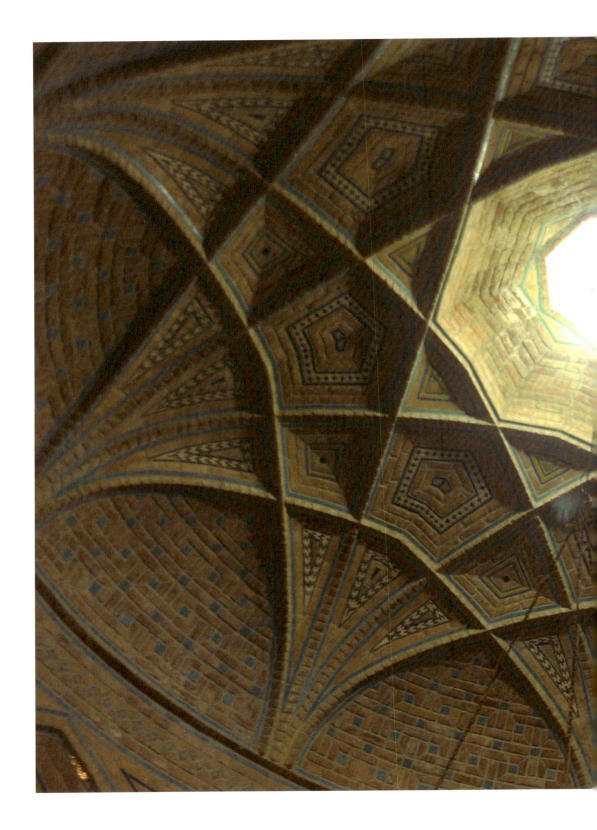

REHABILITATION OF TABRIZ BAZAAR
Tabriz, Iran

In many Eastern countries, ancient bazaars still play a vital role in the community, as they have down the centuries, acting as major economic, social and cultural reference points and influencing the urban fabric and political life. As well as being one of the largest brick complexes in the world, Tabriz Bazaar is one of the oldest in the region. Covering 27 hectares with 5.5 kilometres of inner lanes and counting 5500 shopkeepers and 40 professional guilds, it is the largest covered bazaar in the world in terms of both size and trader numbers. Along with its shops, it includes a variety of functional spaces, such as caravanserais, *timcheh* (domed crossroad nodes), mosques, schools, bathhouses, public squares, gateways and outside green spaces bordering the river.

Settled since 2000 BC, Tabriz is the largest and most important city in the north-east of Iran, located on a vast plain at a high altitude, – surrounded by mountains on three sides, and a lake on the fourth – with a semi-arid climate of short summers and long cold winters. Its monumental Bazaar has signalled the city's greatness over the centuries as a crossroad of ancient civilisations, connecting east to west and north to south, from China to Europe and from Egypt to Russia. It was one of the great destinations along the Silk Road already in Ilkhanid times and many travellers, including Marco Polo, have written about the Bazaar's architectural glories, which enjoyed its heyday in the 16th century when the city was capital of the Safavid dynasty.

The present Bazaar is 230 or so years old, having been almost completely demolished by the disastrous earthquake of 1780 (indeed, ongoing archaeological excavations as part of this project reveal that the Bazaar met this fate a number of times in its long history). By the late 20th century, however, its brick buildings were crumbling due to decades of neglect, businesses were vacating and a local governor had scheduled it for demolition to make way for a new modern market. This situation began to be redressed in the mid-1990s under the auspices of Iran's Cultural Heritage, Handicrafts and Tourism Organisation (ICHTO) with the direct involvement of the traders in all decision-making. This resulted in a successful pilot restoration project that was decisive in winning over all 5500 shopkeepers to the advantages ensuing from an overall rehabilitation project that would conserve and revitalise the valuable heritage of the Bazaar.

After traditional self-management of the Bazaar had been firmly reinstated, a conservation master plan for the entire complex was drafted through a bottom-up grassroots participatory process. ICHTO provided planning and technical assistance and ensured that restoration standards were met. A multi-disciplinary team was set up including engineers to advise on consolidating the stone foundations and reinforcing load-bearing walls and domes in light of Iran's seismic activity, and this remarkable effort of stakeholder coordination and collaboration to restore and bring back to life an essential part of the city could begin.

The sophisticated brickwork throughout – hallmark of the Bazaar – combines both structure and ornament and proved to be a challenging training ground for current experts in restoration who learned in the field from local masons as it was repaired, using traditional techniques. The unique vaulting and domes present intricate geometries and the domed nodal crossroads combine spatial importance with other space-covering geometries. Brick is used for walls, columns and arches too, as well as for the flooring of areas trading in the more expensive goods. As a material, it offers excellent thermal protection in both winter and summer while openings in vaults and domes (some acting as wind-catchers) provide dynamic airflow and sufficient natural light to interior spaces. In comparison with the amount of brick, wood is used more sparingly, mainly as a structural support – apart from majestic doors in the main gates.

Although such a complex will necessarily change over time in line with new requirements, these changes must be well integrated into the whole. For example, today, goods arrive in huge containers rather than in camel-size packs. Consequently areas were created to respond to this new need by placing delivery zones outside the Bazaar and away from its tiny streets, leaving the original inner open spaces for public planted gardens and courtyards. Conversely the random creation of additional mezzanines, hiding traditional ceilings, and the haphazard insertion in the past of concrete structures or utilities, such as air conditioning, into areas where shops or sections had collapsed had to be addressed. It was vital to maintain the Bazaar's highly efficient layout and circulation patterns, evolved over time to meet the needs of shopkeepers and customers through specialised linear streets and major nodal crossings, although gateways and entrances were more clearly identified to facilitate access and emergency routes were created to ease evacuation; new gates were also made, improving connections with the vehicular and pedestrian networks outside and permitting security points and fire service points to be included.

Today, the Bazaar is no longer a place of decaying disorder and insecurity but has once again claimed its position as the dynamic urban centre of the city of Tabriz; shopkeepers have returned; trades on the brink of disappearing have been revived; and the community gathers here in the evenings to socialise. And since being recognised by UNESCO as a World Heritage Site in 2010, it has earned additional international value that will attract foreign tourists.

JURY CITATION

The Rehabilitation of Tabriz Bazaar, with its 5500 shops, is a remarkable example of stakeholder coordination and cooperation to restore and revitalise a unique structure. The architecture of the Bazaar is essentially brick: a singular monolithic material turned into structural and ornamental poetry. The principal expression is the unique vaulting, coordinating light, climate, structure and ornament. The structure that we see dates back 240 years but the site as a place of trade has its origins as far back as the 10th century. It is considered one of the largest brick complexes in the world. What the collaboration, under the direction of the design team, managed to achieve is to return to prominence a historic and living city artefact to the centre of the community's lives.

The project has contributed to the revival and transfer of lost building techniques and skills and has shed light on an important model of this essential everyday typology that challenges us about the quality of commercial space. It is a great reference and example of high-quality architecture and living urban fabric that is still in use as originally intended.

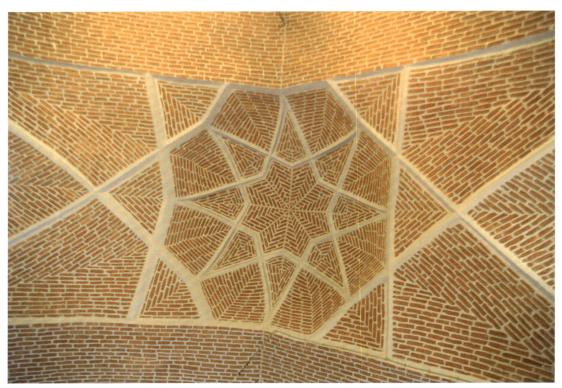

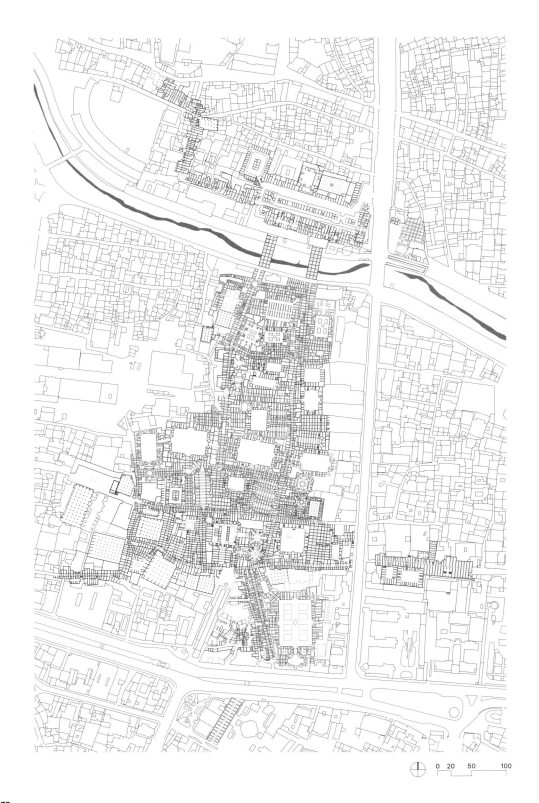

REHABILITATION OF TABRIZ BAZAAR
Tabriz, Iran

CLIENTS
Iran Cultural Heritage, Handicrafts and Tourism Organisation of East Azerbaijan Province, Tabriz, Iran

Bazaar Community, Tabriz, Iran

COMMUNITY ORGANISERS
Haji Hashem Madineie, Ahmad Khadem Hosseini, Tabriz, Iran

ARCHITECT
Iran Cultural Heritage, Handicrafts and Tourism Organisation of East Azerbaijan Province, Tabriz, Iran:
Farhad Tehrani, director (1980s)
Abdoulrahman Vahabzadeh, director (1980–93)
Akbar Taghizadeh Asl, director (1993–2004)
Behrouz Omrani, Saed Hodayi, deputies
Hassan Ghorayshi, architect

CONSULTING ENGINEER
Sakhtab Consulting Engineers, Tehran, Iran

SITE ENGINEERS
Majid Chatrouz, Ghassem Ellmieh, Hossein Esmaili Atigh, Hosein Esmaili Sangari, Tabriz, Iran

ETHNOGRAPHICAL STUDIES
Ali Falsafi, Tabriz, Iran

MASTER MASONS
Hassan Namaki Nasab, Saadollah Doustar, Jalil Abbasi, Allahverdi Ahmadpour, Tabriz, Iran

ADVISOR
Reza Memaran (1993–96), Tabriz, Iran

PROJECT DATA
Site area: 27 ha
Lane length: 5.5 km
Cost: n/a
Commission: 1994–ongoing
Occupancy: 2005–ongoing

IRAN CULTURAL HERITAGE, HANDICRAFTS AND TOURISM ORGANISATION
The establishment of the Iran Cultural Heritage Organisation in 1986 brought together a majority of the public sector institutions involved in cultural activities under one umbrella by merging 11 research and cultural organisations. Two decades later it evolved into the Iran Cultural Heritage, Handicrafts and Tourism Organisation (ICHTO), with a brief to assure that tourism acts in the service of culture and not vice-versa. It covers various fields such as museums, antiquities, archaeology, conservation and restoration of historical monuments and anthropology, and has numerous research centres and bases around the country. ICHTO has a major role in promoting the built heritage through listing buildings, nominating them for inscription on the World Heritage List where appropriate, creating laws and by-laws, and educating experts. The ICHTO of East Azerbaijan is responsible for the conservation and restoration of architectural heritage in the province and its capital, Tabriz, amongst its activities.

AKBAR TAGHIZADEH
Akbar Taghizadeh, a native of Tabriz, after graduating from Shahid Beheshti University in Tehran, began his career with the Iranian Cultural Heritage Organisation, whose approach to cultural heritage was one of revitalising historic monuments rather than of just restoring them, at a time when post-war development plans were already threatening them. During his time at ICHTO in East Azerbaijan from 1993 to 2004, a number of such buildings were successfully brought back to life in the province, such as the restoration and adaptive reuse of various Qajar-era buildings into faculties of architecture and art, a museum on nomads, and a museum on the literature and mysticism of the Qajar era. As the director of the Pardisan Project, Akbar Taghizadeh was responsible for the restoration of a number of historic monuments along the Silk Routes in Iran for reuse as restaurants or guest houses. He is currently engaged in the private sector, active in the rehabilitation of historic monuments in Tehran, Kashan and Kerman.

RABAT-SALÉ URBAN INFRASTRUCTURE PROJECT
Rabat and Salé, Morocco

Standing side by side on the shores of the Atlantic Ocean, which forms Morocco's western border, the two cities of Rabat and Salé, increasingly dependent on one another, are separated by the Bouregreg River, which creates the 6000-hectare, 15-kilometre-wide valley comprising their hinterlands as it penetrates further into the country. In 2003, a special commission was formed to study the area with a view to large-scale regeneration and its far-reaching conclusions signalled a new stage in the history of the valley, socially, economically and urbanistically. The Hassan II Bridge, with its provision for vehicular, tram and pedestrian links between the two cities, was born out of this new vision, since improved transportation and mobility were to be priority components of the larger urban plan, generating the specific infrastructure projects that would have the most significant and immediate impact on the populations of Rabat-Salé.

The two cities meet the river at different levels. The medina of Rabat hangs over the cliff at about 60 metres above water level on the south-western side and the Kasbah des Oudayas district rises up and then descends to meet the seashore at its tip. Other significant historic sites on this bank include the prominently visible Hassan Tower and the Mohammed V Mausoleum, as well as the ancient site of Chellah, which contains ruins of a Roman town. The Salé medina, with ruins dating back to Phoenician times and still to be excavated, rises only 10 metres or so above the level of the north-eastern bank, where the historic monuments of Sidi Ben Achir's Tomb and an aqueduct are located.

Rabat, already declared the civic/administrative capital of Morocco in 1913 under French occupation, is, today, home to the ministries, luxury hotels and residences that befit a capital city, far removed from its 17th-century image of a corsairs' base for waging war against Christians from Spain and Portugal. It covers almost 9530 hectares, and 75% of its population is employed in government administration and support functions. On the other hand, Salé serves as a dormitory town, with the vast majority of its population commuting to Rabat: over 50% of the 400,000 people who travel daily between the two cities were using the old Moulay Hassan Bridge, nearing the end of its design life. It was vital to overcome the physical and socio-economic rift between the cities created by the river and paucity of traffic links and to improve urban well-being by relieving this commuter congestion and pollution. To this end, several new projects were identified and many are now underway (for example, the new Bouregreg Marina, operational since March 2008, and a mixed-use real-estate project of 512,000 square metres called Bab al-Bahr, both on the Salé bank, in the vicinity of the new bridge).

Foremost amongst these projects is the Hassan II Bridge and its associated access structures, designed by French architect Marc Mimram after an invited competition, and built to replace the old Moulay Hassan Bridge, which was kept operative during construction before being demolished. The 46-metre-wide, 330-metre-long Hassan II Bridge, providing vehicular, tram and pedestrian routes, also includes the 600-metre-long Salé viaduct and a tramway access ramp and slip roads at one end, before curving into the 100-metre-long nautical base bridge on the Rabat side at the other, as it extends well into the urban fabric on both sides of the river for a total of 1200 metres. Efficiently linking Carrefour de Kardona in Salé to Place Sidi Makhlouf in Rabat, the Bridge creates covered and open spaces for future public activities at either end of it, thus embracing wider-scale notions of urban planning.

Designed attentively to be "of the place" and "connected to the social landscape and to the people" – in the words of the architect – and so going well beyond the merely engineering aspects of the construction, the Bridge lies low over the river, fully respecting its markedly horizontal context and allowing the historic Hassan Tower to stand proud while impacting as an elegant eye-catching landmark in its own right, with its subtly varied, delicately arched spans and fluid geometry. Designed as three different structural systems in response to the site, the longest 76-metre-clear span of the central portion is formed by an arch section that supports the deck. The Bridge is divided into three separate carriageways on the same level, each supported by structural arches: one for the tramway, and the other two for vehicular traffic. Separate decks are maintained over the regular, shorter spans of the Salé viaduct but united as the asymmetrical structure curves into the nautical base bridge on the Rabat side. The construction solution combined both post-tensioned and prestressed, precast elements and required high technology. The construction system was the first to use very strong prestressed concrete to cope with the forces predicted, and was handled by the local labour force with exemplary skill. The concrete and formwork were also sourced locally.

Opened in 2011, the two tram lines are much appreciated by the community; vehicular flow is much improved; and the walkways offering marvellous views have become a popular destination in their own right: overall quality of life is consequently much enhanced. A successful outcome of the combination of exemplary bridge design, infrastructure improvement and urban planning, the Hassan II Bridge has already become a new iconic symbol of Rabat-Salé, reinforcing their modern, progressive, twin-city identity and laying a sound basis for future infrastructure development.

JURY CITATION

The promise generated by the new Hassan II Bridge anticipates a long-term vision of the cities of Rabat and Salé. Its planning provides opportunities for future development and successfully combines a bridge design with urban planning, landscape and infrastructure improvements. The dynamic complexity of time-based planning is coordinated in multiple layers, providing immediate improvements as well as incremental developments and future opportunities. The ambition of the designer challenges the ordinary boundary of transportation infrastructure and engineering by extending the Bridge beyond the river banks and creating a space for future public activity. The project is a sophisticated and cohesive model for future infrastructure projects, especially in places of rapid urbanisation.

The Bridge profile is low, acting as an impressive horizontal extension of an existing flat plateau, presenting respectful views of the Hassan Tower. Built with great care and high quality of detailing and construction precision, the Bridge has a thin profile and elegant, fluid geometry. It is a pivotal icon, reinforcing the identity of the place, and symbolises a new progressive future for the twin cities.

2013 AWARD RECIPIENT

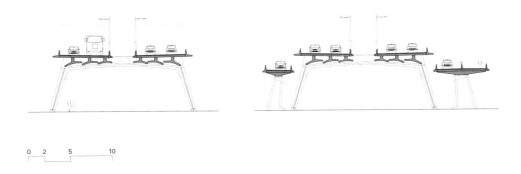

RABAT-SALÉ URBAN INFRASTRUCTURE PROJECT
Rabat and Salé, Morocco

CLIENT
Agence pour l'Aménagement de la Vallée du Bouregreg, Rabat, Morocco:
Lemghari Essakl, director general
Saïd Zarrou, former director of infrastructures
Nada El Kasmi, director of infrastructures
Hassan Mahfoudi, chief engineer of bridge project
Tarik El Idrissi, chief engineer of viaduct project
Mehdi Ouguerd, chief engineer of roadway projects

ARCHITECT
Marc Mimram Architectes, Paris, France:
Marc Mimram, project manager
Nathalie Kreib, Aldo Turchetti, Sergio Pauletto, Nicolas Videgrain, Fabien Mauduit, project team

ENGINEER
Marc Mimram Ingénierie, Paris, France:
Marc Mimram, project manager
Jacques Durst, Razvan Ionica, Arnaud Delugeard, Laurent Becker, project team

ASSOCIATE PROJECT MANAGER
CID (Conseil Ingénierie Développement), Rabat, Morocco:
Moncef Ziani, Fouad Bouklou, Taib Bensied, Chakib Lahjomri

CONTRACTORS
SGTM, Casablanca, Morocco:
Ahmed Kabbaj, director
Serge Bisson, project director
Youssef Kriem, assistant project director

SOGEA Maroc, Rabat, Morocco

DETAILED DESIGN
Hassan II Bridge:
Egis JMI, Saint Quentin en Yvelines, France: Michel Duviard

Nautical Base Bridge:
T-Ingénierie, Geneva, Switzerland:
Jean-François Klein

Freyssinet International, Velizy Villacoublay, France: Jean Pierre Buys

Salé Viaduct and Tram Platform under Rabat's Cliff:
SOGEA, Rabat, Morocco: François Panafieu, Arnaud Warcholak

Tramway Platform and Rabat Bridge Abutment:
TEAM MAROC, Rabat, Morocco: Hicham Hidsi

SECOA, Nanterre, France: Bertrand Lenoir

CONSULTANT
Corrosion Engineering, Annecy, France

PROJECT DATA
Total length: 1030 m
Hassan II Bridge global length: 330 m
Nautical Base Bridge global length: 100 m
Cost: 130,680,000 USD
Commission: May 2006
Design: January 2007–December 2007
Construction: January 2008–May 2011
Occupancy: May 2011

MARC MIMRAM
Born in Paris, France, in 1955, Marc Mimram holds a Master's Degree in Mathematics and graduated as an engineer from the École Nationale des Ponts et Chaussées. He is also an architect (DPLG) and holds a Master's Degree in Civil Engineering from the University of Berkeley in California, in addition to a post-graduate degree in Philosophy.
He founded his own consultancy and architecture-engineering firm in 1981 and has completed a large number of civil engineering structures and architectural projects in France and abroad. Marc Mimram taught at the École Nationale des Ponts et Chaussées, at the École Polytechnique Fédérale de Lausanne, and at Princeton University (USA). He was appointed as Professor of Architectural Schools and currently teaches at the École d'Architecture de Marne-la-Vallée near Paris.

WEBSITES
www.bouregreg.com
www.mimram.com

ISLAMIC CEMETERY
Altach, Austria

Vorarlberg state in western Austria is home to a thriving Muslim community that counts for 10% of the local population, constituting the second largest religious group after the Catholic faith. This Muslim community came to the industrialised state of Vorarlberg for a variety of reasons: in the 1960s, Turkish migrant workers being the predominant group; in the 1990s, Bosnian Muslims who sought refuge in Austria during the Yugoslav wars; and in the last two decades, immigrants from Chechnya, from various North African countries and from South-East Asia. In 2012, Austria celebrated the 100th jubilee of its "Islamic law", issued in 1912 following the Austro-Hungarian annexation of Bosnia and Herzegovina. This law recognised Sunni (Hanafi) Muslims as a religious community and guaranteed them the same religious rights as those of the Empire's other recognised religions. Though the Islamic community in Austria has had a long history, only recently have burials according to the Islamic rite become possible. The Islamic Cemetery in Altach is the first constructed in the Austrian state of Vorarlberg, and the second to be constructed in Austria (the first was built in Vienna in 2008). And, in contrast to the cemetery in Vienna, which serves only the city, it is open to Muslims of all Islamic denominations from all of Vorarlberg's 96 municipalities, so crossing municipal boundaries and giving them equal rights to be buried according to Islamic rituals. Prior to this, Muslims – especially first and second generation – used to send their dead back to their countries of origin (a long, costly and bureaucratically complex process) or opt for burial in extensions of existing cemeteries – such as Vienna, Linz, Innsbruck, Graz and so on – but without full Islamic burial rites. However, by the 1990s, people wanted to stay in Vorarlberg: they had been born here, had married here, had had children here, and so naturally also wanted to be buried here. Highly indicative on many levels of the shifting relationship between Muslim immigrants and the dominant society in their adopted country were the words spoken by the president of the Austrian Islamic Religious Community during the 2012 inaugural ceremony of Altach's Islamic Cemetery: "Homeland is the place where we would like to find our final resting place".

The initial idea for an Islamic cemetery was born in autumn 2003, then followed by years of participatory discussions between Islamic communities and immigrant associations in Vorarlberg on the one hand and the Vorarlberg Association of Municipalities on the other (since cemeteries fall under the jurisdiction of local authorities), culminating in 2008 with the Association buying an 8500-square-metre plot of land that the municipality of Altach had voluntarily proposed for the construction of an Islamic cemetery. The site stands on the local road between the villages of Hohenems and Götzis among rolling green meadows dotted with traditional and contemporary timber architecture, surrounded by spruce forests clothing the mountain faces of the Alps.

Local architect Bernardo Bader was selected after an invited competition to design the building and the site. He was assisted by a community group knowledgeable about the construction of Islamic cemeteries, and by Vorarlberg imams on matters of ritual. Inspired by notions of the primordial garden, a lattice-like system of red concrete walls of varying heights and patterned by formwork delineates five distinct, staggered, grave fields oriented towards Mecca and a rectangular one-storey building in a simple but monumental design. The overall concept features an ingeniously laid out, open plan: towards the road, higher walls provide a feeling of enclosure; towards the mountains, walls are lower and embedded in the ground; everywhere, though, they are broken and interrupted, encouraging a continuous flow of space and dialogue with the surrounding landscape.

The tripartite division, visible on the monumentally "plain" entrance elevation of the Cemetery, gives little indication of the functional spaces within: in the "blind" entrance section, a top-lit mortuary and washroom for the dead and other less used service areas; a covered, half-open gathering area for larger numbers at the centre of the structure – signalled on the exterior by a wooden latticework screen of strong geometric patterns (an abstract reference to both Islamic design and traditional local woodcraft) – that leads directly onto an open patio connecting with the grave fields outside; and a prayer hall in the other "blind" end that has a large window on the short side facing Mecca. In the prayer hall, faced in white-stained wood, Azra Akšamija, a Bosnian-born Austrian Muslim architect and artist, working in close collaboration with Bader, designed the *qibla* wall of three stainless-steel mesh curtains that hang parallel at different distances to the end wall. Hung with an array of wooden shingles, placed more or less densely with some bearing Kufic calligraphic script that spell out the words "Allah" and "Mohammed", these curtains act as screens breaking up the light in dramatic patterns while also referencing the wood shingle walls of local architectural tradition. Throughout, the work was executed by local craftsmen.

The subtle simplicity of the Cemetery's design and its interaction with its natural surroundings provide a calm and dignified place for spiritual contemplation, burial and mourning. Architecturally, it offers a new, culturally sensitive aesthetic that is both Islamic and Alpine. This pioneering project has successfully responded to an immigrant community's desire to find a final resting place in its adopted homeland, triggering interest in other Austrian states to create similar facilities.

JURY CITATION

The Islamic Cemetery, in its restrained and measured expression, belies a complex cultural negotiation. In the context of its host environment, it presents a symbolically charged site as a place of resolve. The project brought together a multi-faith, multi-ethnic group of actors to realise the wish of an immigrant community seeking to create a space that fulfils their spiritual aspirations and, at the same time, responds to the context of their adopted country with a culturally sensitive design and aesthetic.

Simple in expression and poetic in form, it not only engages the natural landscape in an intelligent manner but also suspends any notion of declaration. While emphasising spiritual pluralism, the Cemetery also provides the final destination for a minority group in a dominant society.

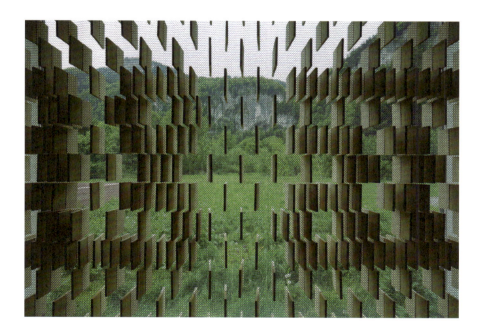

2013 AWARD RECIPIENT

ISLAMIC CEMETERY
Altach, Austria

CLIENT
Municipality of Altach, Altach, Austria: Gottfried Brändle, Mayor of Altach, Austria

ARCHITECT
Bernardo Bader, Dornbirn, Austria

CONSULTANTS
Eva Grabherr, director of Okay.zusammen leben/Advice Centre for Immigration and Integration, Dornbirn, Austria

Vorarlberg Association of Municipalities, Dornbirn, Austria

Attila Dincer, leader of the initiatory group "Islamic Cemetery", Dornbirn, Austria

ARTIST
Azra Akšamija, Boston, USA

STRUCTURAL ENGINEER
Merz Kley Partner ZT GmbH, Dornbirn, Austria: Gordian Kley, partner

SITE SUPERVISOR
Thomas Marte, Dornbirn, Austria

CRAFTSMEN
Association for the Preservation of the Bosnian Kilim, Sarajevo, Bosnia and Herzegovina

PROJECT DATA
Site area: 8415 m^2
Built area: 468 m^2
Cost: 2,983,000 USD
Commission: June 2008
Design: January 2008–December 2011
Construction: March 2010–December 2011
Occupancy: December 2011

BERNARDO BADER
Bernardo Bader is an architect from Krumbach, the Austrian region of Bregenzerwald, currently with an office in Dornbirn, Austria. He studied architecture at the Innsbruck Technical University and, after receiving his engineering degree (Dipl. Ing.) in 2001, he founded his own architectural office. His work investigates how architecture can be embedded in regional building culture, based on local architectural grammar. His projects bear witness to the excellence of handcraft, deep attention to tectonic detail and sensitivity to the local context. Bader is a member of the Advisory Design Commissions as well as the Advisory Committee for Urban Contemplation in the Vorarlberg region. Since 2012, he has held a lecturing position at the University of Liechtenstein in Vaduz. He has received a number of prestigious awards, including the Weissenhof Architectural Furtherance Prize 2007 for young architects in Stuttgart, Germany, the Constructive – Liechtenstein Prize for sustainable building in 2011, the Piranesi Award 2013, and numerous local timber construction awards, as well as clients' awards. His work was nominated for the DETAIL Prize 2012 and the Mies van der Rohe Award 2013.

WEBSITE
www.bernardobader.com

SALAM CENTRE FOR CARDIAC SURGERY
Khartoum, Sudan

Before the cessation of South Sudan in 2011, Sudan was the largest country in Africa. Khartoum, the capital, is located in the central part, close to the confluence of the Blue and White Niles, with an estimated population of about five million (reputedly increased by a further three when the informal camps and settlements established in the city by refugees fleeing internal conflict are taken into account). Almost half have no access to water and more than half have no access to sanitation in a city that is one of the hottest in the world, with summer temperatures over 50 °C and very little rain even in the wet season. The area is also beset by frequent desert sandstorms that reduce visibility to zero and render the air unbreathable. The most recent figures of the Human Development Index – used to calculate an accepted broad definition of well-being in terms of health, education and income – rank Sudan just above war-torn countries such as Afghanistan, Liberia and Mali.

In 2004, Emergency – a small independent Italian NGO founded in 1994, acting primarily to provide free, high-quality medical and surgical treatment for victims of war, landmines and poverty – chose to bring its skills to the country: the Salam Centre for Cardiac Surgery was one of the projects it set up. With the help of the Sudanese government and especially the Ministry of Health, a plot of about 14,000 square metres on the east bank of the Blue Nile in Soba, a suburb 20 kilometres from Khartoum and once the Coptic capital of Sudan (AD 540–1604), was allocated for the construction of the new facility, which today offers free-of-charge treatment to people with congenital or acquired heart pathologies. Cardiovascular diseases, mainly deriving from rheumatic fever that is widespread in the region and that predominately affects children and adolescents, cause 10% of deaths in Sudan and neighbouring countries.

The inspiring words of Gino Strada, surgeon and founder of Emergency, informed the project from the start: "We want our hospital to be beautiful, 'scandalously beautiful', because that beauty becomes a token of respect towards people devastated by war or disease and a beautiful place offers the conditions essential to regaining dignity in suffering. For this reason, in all our hospitals the utmost importance is attached to children's playrooms, social spaces and gardens. Treatment is not confined to operating theatres and wards only, but applied through care devoted to each person as an absolute human being."

Essentially a "self-build" project managed by Emergency, the Salam Centre was designed and delivered by the team of Italian architects of studio tamassociati working on a not-for-profit basis. Wherever possible, construction was contracted to local builders and suppliers, while the specialised medical equipment was gifted as charitable donations from international sources. The main buildings of the complex are the central, one-storey, highly technical hospital pavilion (three theatres, 63 beds, diagnostic wing), flanked by a guest house for relatives and smaller separate service buildings, the prayer and meditation pavilion, a solar panel facility, and the medical staff accommodation compound (sleeping 150), all set within a large well-kept garden and around large grassy, planted and shaded courtyards.

The main challenge for the architects was the intense heat. The orientation of the plot was exploited to combat this, extensive use was made of large shade trees in the outdoor areas, and linking paths were screened with traditional panels of intertwined vegetable fibres, while a double-shell system for walls and roofs was devised to keep the buildings cool. This resulted in a "box within a box" structure for the hospital block, with a large void above the ceiling protected by an insulated metal outer skin, while 60-centimetre-thick cavity walls with insulated panels were made from locally fired bricks, providing an effective low-tech thermal barrier All windows are sunscreen coated and double glazed. Air conditioners powered by a barrage of solar panels circulate the 28,000 cubic metres of cold air needed every hour and help maintain constant satisfactory indoor temperatures. A "sand trap" in the basement sucks in dust-laden sandstorm air, removes the sand and passes the clean, cooler air into the ventilation system. Water is obtained from deep aquifer wells pumped into a cleansing system and power is supplied by the grid, although back-up generators are on hand. Self-sufficiency and sustainability are, indeed, hallmarks of this state-of-the-art hospital's design, coupled of course with "beauty", all tailored to the human dimension, making it a welcoming yet highly efficient, holistic, multi-faith environment, with natural light, views outside, clear layout and signage, cheerful colours and greenery.

Recycling also plays a major role, most clearly demonstrated in the reuse of 95 six-metre containers as residential units and communal areas in the staff compound. Each unit – again insulated by a double-shell system plus bamboo brise-soleil panels – contains a bathroom and small veranda onto the garden and was made from one and a half containers set against each other around two planted courtyards. The prayer and meditation pavilion was sensitively designed to be a peaceful space welcoming all religions: two interconnected cubic volumes on shallow water.

The Salam Centre has had a tremendous impact, treating significant numbers of patients not only from Sudan and its neighbours, but from a good 23 other countries as well. In addition, people come to train here and, most importantly, its example and vision have encouraged the establishment of further medical centres of excellence in other African countries.

JURY CITATION
The Salam Centre for Cardiac Surgery champions the vision and resilience of all involved in delivering a responsible, efficient and inspiring model of health services in a society marred by war, internal conflict and lack of basic needs like water and sanitation.

Intimately linked to surrounding nature, the "self-build" project facilitates an environment of clarity and healing, while providing the fundamental human right of health, free of charge to all. Following a bottom-up design process, this complex project evolved successfully by creatively engaging all its local, political, social, topographical and aesthetic specificities without sacrificing its vision for excellence and function. The compact state-of-the-art hospital also provides an exemplary prototype for the region as well as for the field.

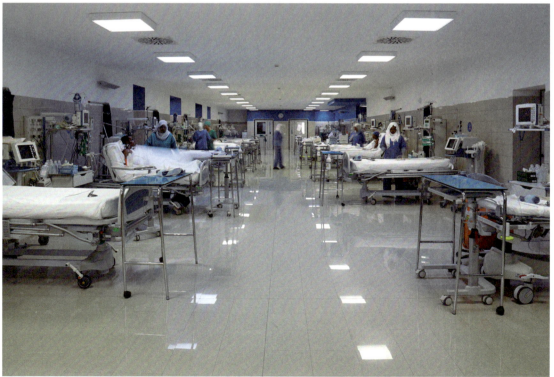

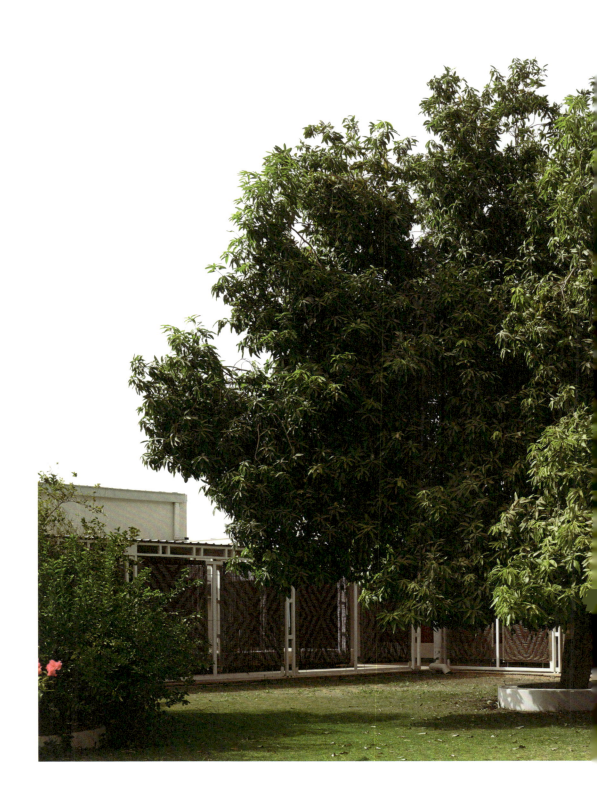

2013 AWARD RECIPIENT

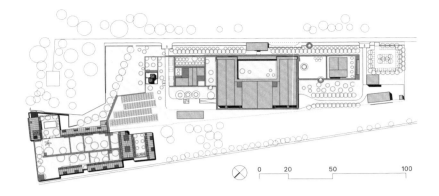
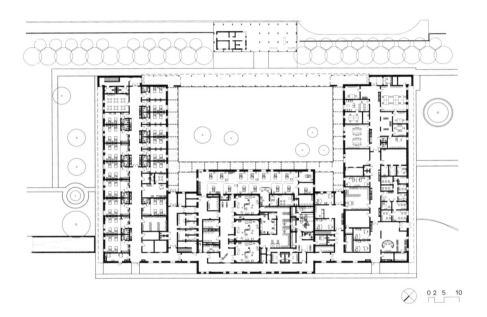
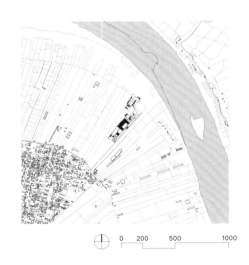

SALAM CENTRE FOR CARDIAC SURGERY
Khartoum, Sudan

CLIENT
Emergency, Milan, Italy:
Gino Strada, founder

TOTAL SITE AREA
40,000 m²

HOSPITAL BLOCK

ARCHITECT
Studio Tamassociati, Venice, Italy:
Raul Pantaleo, Massimo Lepore, Simone Sfriso design team with Sebastiano Crescini
Pietro Parrino, project manager and programme coordinator
Rossella Miccio, programme coordinator
Francesco Steffinlongo, structural engineer
Studio Pasquini, Jean Paul Riviere with Nicola Zoppi, mechanical/services engineer
Franco Binetti, operating theatre design
Roberto Crestan with Alessandro Giacomello, site engineer
Gino Strada, Emiliano Cinelli, Fabrizio Fasano, Andrea Cioffi, feasibility project

PROJECT DATA
Built area: 21,500 m²
Cost: 18,452,000 USD
Commission: December 2004
Design: December 2004–May 2007
Construction: January 2005–May 2007
Occupancy: May 2007

MEDICAL STAFF ACCOMMODATION COMPOUND

ARCHITECT
Studio Tamassociati, Venice, Italy:
Raul Pantaleo, Massimo Lepore, Simone Sfriso, design team
Pietro Parrino, programme coordinator
Francesco Steffinlongo, structural engineer
Nicola Zoppi, mechanical/services engineer
Roberto Crestan, Alessandro Tamai, Claudio Gatti, site engineers

PROJECT DATA
Built area: 2400 m²
Cost: 1,367,000 USD
Commission: March 2006
Design: March 2006
Construction: December 2007–February 2009
Occupancy: February 2009

EMERGENCY
Emergency is an Italian NGO founded in 1994 by the Italian surgeon, Dr Gino Strada, to provide assistance to civilian victims of war. From 1994, Emergency has worked in 16 countries, building hospitals, surgical centres, rehabilitation centres, paediatric clinics, first-aid posts, primary health clinics and a maternity centre, as well as the Centre for Cardiac Surgery in Khartoum. Subsequent to requests from local authorities and other organisations, Emergency has also helped to renovate and equip pre-existing health facilities. Since 1994, Emergency teams have provided assistance to 5,439,757 people (as of 31 March 2013).

STUDIO TAMASSOCIATI
Studio Tamassociati is a professional practice active in the fields of sustainable architecture, urban planning, landscape design, participatory processes, graphic design and social communications. It comprises an Italian team of architects based in Venice since 1996 and it is known worldwide for health-care works carried out on the African continent.
In 2012, the project was awarded the Honourable Mention in the category "Architecture for Emergency" at the Gold Medal for Italian Architecture Prize, Triennale of Milan, Italy, following other international awards such as "Best of Green Awards" 2010 (USA) and "Middle East Architect Awards" 2010 (Dubai). Main recent exhibitions include "2012 Triennale of Architecture", Milan, Italy, and exhibitions and lectures at the "International Biennale of Architecture" in 2010 and 2012, Venice, Italy.

WEBSITES
www.salamcentre.emergency.it
www.emergency.it
www.tamassociati.org

PLACENESS AND WELL-BEING, THROUGH THE LENS OF INFRASTRUCTURE
Hanif Kara

INTRODUCTION
In the context of the Aga Khan Award for Architecture one could simply characterise infrastructure projects as physical systems that are essential in sustaining an advancing society in a productive way while protecting nature, enhancing societal living conditions and improving the "quality of life". Infrastructure and urban design are siblings; cities and their buildings are rooted in both. The projects selected in this cycle present an opportunity to give infrastructure more visibility and prominence. Often infrastructure stands in the background, hidden from view, its value apparent only to those intimately involved in designing or commissioning it. More often than not citizens only become aware of its existence when something goes wrong, such as the damage caused by the earthquake in Sichuan province, Hurricane Katrina, the Gulf of Mexico oil spill, or flight delays at snow-bound terminals.

Though the term infrastructure has broader meanings (land-based and institutional), it typically refers to technical systems such as water supply, roads, bridges, tunnels, schools, airports and hospitals. Multidisciplinary design professionals engaged with the built environment including infrastructure therefore play a big part in providing a means of interacting with one's environment to create places that harness the attributes of a landscape and its resources in an efficient way without ignoring the political, cultural, ecological and economical challenges.

THE IMPORTANCE OF HISTORY AND CONTEXT
From the dawn of history the roles of civil engineering and architecture have mirrored the development of human beings on this earth, since man sheltered in caves to protect himself from weather and harsh environments and used tree trunks to cross rivers. Such simple references provide an opportunity to assess, in clear and simpler conditions when we were less obscured by specialisation, the role of the built environment, its professionals, its dependence on technology and its direct correlation with cultural and economical prosperity.

The civilisations of the Nile valley 3000 years ago would not have arisen without the intense cultivation of the land and consequential concentration of populations. In Greece there is evidence of early water supply systems, tunnels and Roman aqueducts, and on roads all over the world the effects of Roman engineering still resonate. Throughout ancient history most architectural design and construction was carried out by artisans:[1] structure and infrastructure were repetitive, simple in scale and incremental. It was not until the 18th century that a scientific approach to physical and mathematical problems arrived. The early 1800s saw the birth of the civil engineer.

The roots of modern planning lie in the industrial cities of the 19th century and their endemic problems of poor sanitation in buildings, coupled with inferior supplies of water, air and light, which affected health and eventually triggered a response; its history can be seen to mirror human development. The discipline's increasing empowerment in the 20th century has caused it in some ways to pay less attention to the ethics of social conditions, political ideologies and theoretical discourse as civil engineers have led infrastructural policy and dominated this area of work. This has often produced quantitative logics,[2] numerical precisions to achieve accuracy and efficiencies, with the softer "design aspects" losing ground through little or no involvement from architects.

To counteract this, an appreciation of how urban environments affect health and can produce health benefits is being researched in some depth under the overarching umbrella of societal "well-being", a phrase somewhat interchangeable with "quality of life". On a practical level, this encompasses an absence of ill health and a growth of prosperity resulting from the physical context within urban environments, including the material fabric of buildings, infrastructure and spatial organisation. Accepted broad definitions for the well-being of a society (the WHO Human Development Index for instance) attempt to measure three dimensions of human development: health, education and income. There is much to say about the interrelationship of the Award and the issues of infrastructure, place-making and well-being, and there are many projects that could be cited from the Aga Khan Award for Architecture's archives that cannot find space in this text. As early as the first cycle, the magnificent Kuwait City Water Towers gained an Award, while more recently in 2010 the Wadi Hanifa Wetlands project in Saudi Arabia, with its impressive bioremediation facility, was awarded. Through the providence of those involved, in 1983 the Hajj Terminal at King Abdul Aziz International Airport in Jedda (the first "transportation project") received an Award. The consensus was that its concept of providing infrastructure in the form of a "pop-up" village (rather than a terminal) capable of handling large volumes of people in a short period during the Muslim pilgrimage, as well as its unique translucent roof, was well executed. Since then a number of such transportation projects have been shortlisted, including the Kuala Lumpur Light Rail Transit (2007) and the impressive Kuala Lumpur International Airport (2007), born out of the prescient vision of Prime Minister Mahathir bin Mohamad to make Malaysia a fully developed industrial nation by 2020.

Whether we take our bearings from general patterns of political science, social equality or the specifics of design excellence, the success of the Salam

Centre for Cardiac Surgery in Sudan in this cycle of the Award defies all the rules of the game. In sharing the values of the Aga Khan Award for Architecture, this well-accomplished project achieved the objective of excellence at many levels, from a poetic reuse of the shipping containers (symbol of globalisation) that had delivered the medical equipment, to the birth of ANME (African Network for Medical Excellence), a cooperation between many countries in the region to emphasise the importance of high-quality health care. The low-level forms of the Centre successfully play "hide and seek" with nature and artificiality to deliver a hospital in a garden, while being scandalously beautiful, unashamedly functional and rooted in the place, politically and socially. These aspects are crucial in a country of infrastructural constraints, where 66% of the population has no access to sanitation, 43% no access to water and a mere 31% can use available health facilities. This facility has succeeded in treating patients not only from Sudan but also from another 23 countries, acting as an infrastructure hub for a network of outreach clinics. At another extreme, the comprehensive Revitalisation of Birzeit Historic Centre in Palestine and the Rehabilitation of Tabriz Bazaar in Iran both brought about a substantial "mending" of the existing infrastructure that will repair whole communities.

The Hassan II Bridge in Morocco, on the other hand, is born out of a wide-ranging study of the Bouregreg Valley that identified the need to connect the two cities of Rabat and Salé with its key urban drivers: the protection of the two historic medinas; the repair of the natural estuary and its landscape; and the decontamination of the Bouregreg River, while making provision for the impact of flooding as a result of climate change. The design of the Bridge blends with the surrounding landscape and medinas, as it grows out of the ground rather than crowds the sky, as would be the case with most bridges. As a symbol of the new capital and the physical infrastructure it provides, the Bridge will unite communities and thus improve the quality of life, as well as provide new jobs that complement the local cultures and context. Most of all, it will become pivotal in encouraging new developments, including urban space planned for beneath the Bridge. The architect deliberately expanded the brief for a purely structural solution for spanning the river and chose to tackle the more difficult urban challenges posed by truly connecting the urban fabric on either bank. As a connector of two communities and a symbol of progress in modern construction in this part of the world, this Bridge sets a new benchmark.

THE IMMEDIATE FUTURE
Sustaining current and future lifestyles has become an increasingly prominent issue among academics, in legislation and practice, particularly since the 1992 Rio Declaration. Amidst this host of economic and environmental challenges, what the winning projects highlight above all is the role that intuitive, carefully conceived high-quality design can play in targeting the needs of both the structure and the people it serves, in a way that is entirely specific

to its context. Each of the winning schemes offers more than just a well-considered form; the infrastructures and buildings are used as a means of connecting cities, renewing communities or providing much-needed health facilities in remote locations. What is apparent in the awarded projects is the benefit of a deeper application of interdisciplinary consideration that is "quality centred" and takes a more integrative lens to synthesise technological, spatial and biophysical conditions with political, cultural, social and economic concerns in place-making through infrastructure.

One approach to encourage this further could be to apply "design thinking", a term used by Tim Brown[3] and others, to effect a change in attitude and bring "design" upstream in the process. In recent times society has been stuck in a culture of consumption, incessant production and prodigious waste. Since the economic crash of 2008 there has been some aggressive belt-tightening, and both the private and public sector have changed their approach to infrastructure. Reduced economic productivity, real-estate demands and global competitive processes are reawakening the importance of infrastructure, as society, both in the developed and less developed world, recognises the need to fund infrastructures together with the need for an "economy centred" approach that requires not only more imagination from designers but also "design thinking".

King Mohammed VI of Morocco will be considered a formidable "design thinker" when his full vision for the redevelopment of the Bouregreg Valley and desire to unite two adjacent cities is realised. His well-conceived intention at policy level recognises that the appointment of "good designers" would, on the one hand, maximise the united cities' productive power and regional influence, and, in parallel, encourage private finance initiatives to assist development of housing and cultural institutions along the river. The Hassan II Bridge in Rabat-Salé would not then be considered in isolation but as a pivotal urban intervention that secures well-being for the community it serves.

The novel vision of NGO Emergency's altruistic leader Gino Strada to prescribe a "scandalously beautiful centre of excellence for cardiac surgery" at the Salam Centre in Sudan, which would not only bring health to an area of deprivation but also act as a driving force in fostering cooperation between 23 countries, makes him a "design thinker" too.

At a time in history when, once again, everybody is in the business of austerity and stability is the new growth, the Jury's selections in this cycle of the Award serve to draw the attention of the wider constituencies of the Aga Khan Award for Architecture to a more optimistic future based on high-quality "design", "design thinking" and investment in infrastructure. For the "search masters" of today and the professional community (and here I am throwing down the gauntlet to engineers and architects), we must post-rationalise these schemes, since, for the most part, infrastructure projects appear to be driving architects and engineers apart again, introducing a tension between art and science; the best projects demonstrate that a "bottom-up" approach with a focus on ethics and compassion can still be used to enrich our work. For scholars, the cornucopia of ideas (technical and beyond) paraded by this cycle, some old and some new, deserves a closer examination that may foster learning from the grassroots of successfully tried and tested places.

1 The Civil Engg Site, (2012) *History of Civil Engineering*. Available at http://www.thecivilengg.com/History.php (accessed on 21 June 2013).

2 Pierre Bélanger, "Landscape Infrastructure: Urbanism beyond Engineering", in N. Spiro (et al.), *Infrastructure Sustainability and Design*, New York: Routledge, 2012, p. 276.

3 Tim Brown, *Change by Design: How Design Thinking Creates New Alternatives for Business and Society: How Design Thinking Transforms Organizations and Inspires Innovation*, New York: Harper Collins, 2009.

INSTITUTION

How do we gather, learn from and disseminate the cultural and social aspirations and order of a community? Projects such as the Lycée Français Charles de Gaulle, Mohammed VI Football Academy and Museum of Handcraft Paper demonstrate the importance of educational, social, cultural and vocational forms of knowledge. These projects exemplify the role of institutions as the emblems of our aspirations.

LYCÉE FRANÇAIS CHARLES DE GAULLE
Damascus, Syria

Set on the slopes of the Mezzah district – once the summer retreat for Damascenes living in the hotter old city in the valley below – the Lycée Charles de Gaulle in Damascus offers a French education for 900 students from kindergarten to baccalaureate level. Inaugurated in 2008, the project aimed to provide an integrated campus for three schools previously located in different buildings in the city. The campus design, with its own strong formal image, is generated to a large extent in response to the physical constraints of the sloping site, the arid desert climate and, crucially, the desire for natural ventilation and sustainability. Indeed, the decision to erect a building in the Middle East without air conditioning came as a surprise to many and, in fact, resulted in the school standing out so clearly from its high-density residential surroundings.

The "garden" is the spatial building block of the overall design scheme and essential to the central strategy for natural cooling and ventilation systems. The classrooms of the three schools – kindergarten and primary on the left and secondary on the right – are arranged in a pattern of alternating pavilions and garden-patios either side of the main axes along a major courtyard leading up the hill.

Each two-storey block is made up of two classrooms with thermal-inducing double-block walls (hollow concrete on the exterior, solid concrete on the interior separated by a 5-centimetre air pocket) and gives onto a small, planted garden-patio that acts as a microclimate providing cool air. This passes through PVC pipes in the ground-floor slabs and circulates via the natural updraft created by the specifically placed, tall solar chimneys – one for each classroom – that give the campus its distinctive image. Each classroom has a dual aspect and the size and position of the double-glazed windows were carefully studied to provide maximum natural light. The patios are planted and/or shaded with retractable awnings and every classroom is connected to the main avenue by a system of open and roofed two-level corridors paved with basalt tiles: again, designed with cooling and ventilation in mind. The aluminium or zinc-clad roofs also provide additional protection and are sloped parallel to the site, facilitating rainwater collection.

To establish the necessary microclimate and garden, great care was taken to preserve all the existing trees, which also frame views to the mountains beyond, and many fast-growing local varieties that require little water were added.

LYCÉE FRANÇAIS CHARLES DE GAULLE
Damascus, Syria

CLIENTS
French Ministry of Foreign Affairs, Paris, France

Parent-Teacher Association for the Charles de Gaulle Senior High School, Damascus, Syria

ARCHITECT
Ateliers Lion Associés, Paris, France:
Yves Lion, principal
Claire Piguet, David Jolly, project team

LOCAL ARCHITECT
Dagher Hanna & Partners, Beirut, Lebanon

STRUCTURAL ENGINEER
GEC Ingénierie, Paris, France

FLUID ENGINEER
Barbanel Liban, Beirut, Lebanon

PEDOLOGICAL STUDIES
Sol Paysage, Paris, France

CLIMATE ENGINEER
Transsolar Energietechnik GmbH, Stuttgart, Germany

PROJECT DATA
Site area: 10,000 m^2
Ground-floor area: 4995 m^2
Cost: 6,576,000 USD
Commission: June 2001
Design: January 2006
Construction: April 2006–May 2008
Completion: September 2008

YVES LION
Yves Lion was born in Casablanca in 1945. He studied architecture in the Pingusson workshop at the École des Beaux Arts and, subsequently, at the University of Paris VI. He established his agency in 1974, and was fully involved in debates and competitions during the period that marked the emergence of "urban architecture".
From the earliest days, he has been involved in social-housing projects. He has also designed numerous housing schemes for private developers, as well as many public buildings, including the Palais de Justice in Lyon (1995) and the French Embassy in Beirut (2003).
His career has been punctuated by other projects involving cultural and educational facilities, including the renovation of the Fine Arts Museum in Dijon, the Paris Institute of Islamic Cultures and the National Institute of Oriental Languages and Civilisations in Paris.
He combines urban design analyses, urban development projects, public spaces and territorial development. He focuses on the creation of links as a means of repairing breaches (between city centres and suburbs), by the reclamation of fallow land or the redevelopment of infrastructures, and on the relationship between townscape and nature.
In 2007, he was awarded the "Grand Prix de l'Urbanisme" prize for urban development and, in 2010, the "Prix National de l'Aménagement Urbain" national urban development prize, together with the Municipality of Strasbourg.

WEBSITE
www.atelierslion.com

MOHAMMED VI FOOTBALL ACADEMY
Salé, Morocco

The Academy provides intensive football training and a school education for about 70 rigorously selected students aged between 13 and 18, and is designed to encourage focus and a sense of community. It is located on a fairly flat agricultural plain on the outskirts of Salé, on the right bank of the Bouregreg River, opposite the capital Rabat. The site covers nearly 12 hectares and is buffered along the road to the north-west by a stand of old eucalyptus trees that were preserved and added to.

Once past this screen, the five buildings of the residential academy are revealed, respectively accommodating administrative, sports, teaching, lodging and catering functions forming a campus. The blocks are arranged like a traditional introverted *douar* (hamlet) around a central "village square", while the football grounds occupy the other half of the site. The concept of the *douar* draws on a sense of belonging to a place that is familiar, secure, comfortable and centred, and the arrangement of the buildings around the central square encourages communication and a clear sense of community.

The buildings present massive plain white walls pierced by varied groupings of carefully placed large or small openings that maximise thermal flows and introduce natural light and views over the open landscape or into the enclosed inner courts. The white facades are also broken up by areas of local ochre-coloured stone that enhance the rhythm of the strong contemporary design and anchor the buildings to the ground. Local skills, methods and materials were used throughout.

In response to climatic conditions, each block is developed around a central landscaped patio, which facilitates ventilation and increases the natural light in the main spaces. In striking contrast to the exterior white, each inner patio is painted a vibrant colour that reflects an aspect of Morocco: ocean blues, fertile-plain greens, southern ochres…

The chromatic moods of these inner courts are designed for relaxation, apart from the life of the "village square", and are enriched by the careful planting of their thematic gardens – a tropical garden, an Andalusian garden, a dry garden. These help to underline the quality and separate identity of these inner spaces whereas the landscaping and careful selection of drought-resistant, low-maintenance planting around the exteriors and in the borders play a major role in tying all the parts of the whole together.

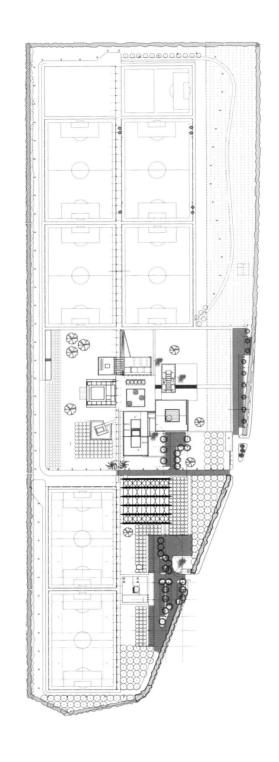

MOHAMMED VI FOOTBALL ACADEMY
Salé, Morocco

CLIENT
Association Mohammed VI de Football, Rabat, Morocco:
Mohcine Benyacoub, president
Nasser Larguet, director

ARCHITECT
Groupe 3 Architectes, Rabat, Morocco:
Omar Tijani, Skander Amine, principal architects

PROJECT MANAGER
Compagnie Générale Immobilière, Rabat, Morocco

LANDSCAPE ARCHITECT
MB Paysage, Rabat, Morocco:
Mounia Bennani

ENGINEER
NOVEC, Rabat, Morocco

PROJECT DATA
Site area: 2,500,000 m^2
Total built area: 9000 m^2
Cost: 15,250,000 USD
Commission: June 2007
Design: June 2007–March 2008
Construction: July 2008–March 2010
Completion: September 2010

GROUPE 3 ARCHITECTES
Groupe 3 Architectes is a Rabat-based architecture firm founded in 2000 by Skander Amine, who graduated from Braunschweig Technical University, Germany, in 1999, and Omar Tijani, who graduated from the Paris-La Villette School of Architecture, France.
The firm has a multidisciplinary and a culturally diverse team of 30 collaborators whose professional expertise is constantly nurtured by the emerging collective intelligence.
Driven by the shared conviction that each project is unique, the firm's partners develop an ambitious vision for each architectural and urban project, and are able to deliver innovative responses in accordance with the urban, social and cultural contexts.
Alongside this qualified team of landscape, facade, acoustics and sustainability specialists, the firm's partners' proposals are built on fully integrated design solutions, and their commitment to research and development has allowed them to bring their combined expertise to bear on a diverse range of projects across the world.

WEBSITES
www.amfoot.ma
www.groupe3architectes.com

MUSEUM OF HANDCRAFT PAPER
Gaoligong, Yunnan, China

Paper was one of the great inventions of the ancient Chinese, dating back to more than 2000 years ago. As its name suggests, the Museum of Handcraft Paper displays the history and processes of paper-making, along with practical demonstrations and workshops. It exhibits, preserves and develops the art of local paper-making and promotes academic research and cultural exchange. To these ends, it also offers accommodation for visitors and artists' residencies and has a tea room that acts as the meeting place for the local village. It can be seen as part of a recent trend in China for small-scale specialised museums dedicated to documenting and making known the country's regional history and culture.

The Museum is located on one side of the road leading to Xingzhuang village, in Yunnan province, surrounded by rapeseed fields and with views to the Gaoligong Mountains in the distance. The timber building is massed in eight irregularly shaped blocks of different heights linked by glazed corridors, creating varied views of the landscape from within and an interesting orchestration of volumes from without: the layout evokes the typical clustering of family houses in the village beyond.

On the ground floor, the largest block houses the main hall and shop and six single-storey exhibition galleries extend out from this on both sides of the central two-storey tea room and terrace outside. A large work area and meeting room topped by accommodation and outdoor terraces complete the upper floors of the three-storey entrance block. The building stands on a base of local volcanic stone that is punctuated with gaps to ensure good cross ventilation throughout. Locally sourced wood was used for the superstructure (made with traditional mortise and tenon joints), for the timber plank finishes on the facades and interior walls (creating cavity walls to aid insulation and temperature control), and for the flooring, windows and doors, all executed by local workmen. Bamboo was laid above timber beams and waterproofed planks to finish the roofing, further enriching the distinctive design of the irregular roof planes. Inside, tilted planes of folded ceilings match up with the non-rectangular walls of the individual galleries, which are sometimes also lined with paper. Paper also covers a number of window openings, letting translucent light into the galleries.

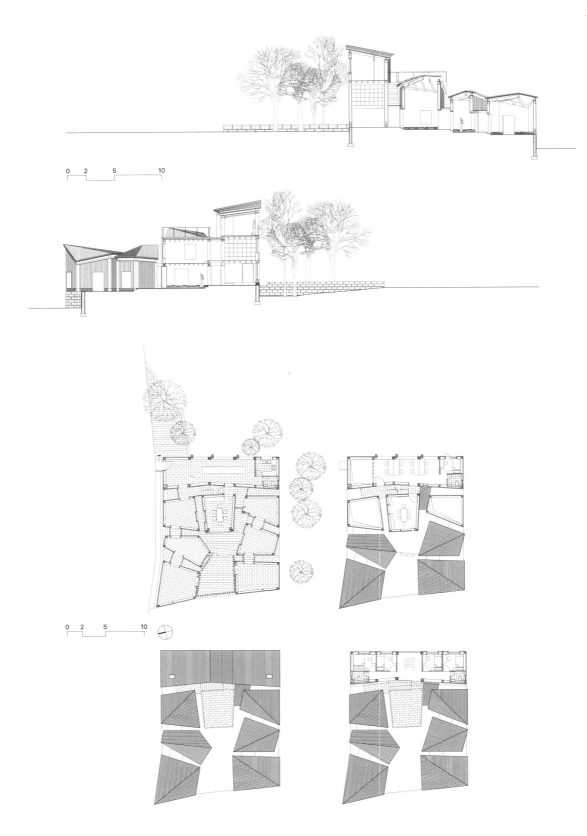

MUSEUM OF HANDCRAFT PAPER
Gaoligong, Yunnan, China

CLIENTS
Long Zhanxian, local paper-making master and museum director, head of Longshang tribe

Long Wen, academic, researcher and scholar, Beijing, China

Wang Yan, product and graphic designer, investor and manager of client, Beijing, China,

ARCHITECT
Trace Architecture Office, Beijing, China:
Hua Li, principal
Huang Tianju, Li Guofa, Jiang Nan, Sun Yuanxia, Xu Yinjun, Yang Hefeng, design team

LEADER OF LOCAL BUILDERS
Long Zhanwen, Xinzhuang Village, Tengchong City, China

PROJECT DATA
Site area: 300 m^2
Total built area: 361 m^2
Cost: 80,820 USD
Commission: April 2008
Design: April 2008–May 2009
Construction: May 2009–December 2010
Completion: December 2010

TAO (TRACE ARCHITECTURE OFFICE)
Founded by Hua Li in 2009, TAO (Trace Architecture Office) is a Beijing-based design studio committed to architecture and urban and landscape design. Being critical of contemporary architecture as obsessed with fancy forms and becoming simply a fashion or dogma in the context of media-driven globalised consumerism, TAO envisions architecture and its environment as an inseparable whole, so that architecture is always part of its surroundings rather than an isolated object. TAO is interested in the specific relationship between the building and its place. With most of their projects located in particular cultural and natural settings in China, TAO aims to make architecture deeply rooted in its social and environmental context. The sense of place, response to climate, efficient use of local resources, appropriate material and construction techniques, such essential issues are always explored in every TAO project, responding to its specific situation.

TAO has focused on institutional and cultural projects, such as museums, schools, hospital buildings and so on. It has realised several award-winning projects, including the Museum of Handcraft Paper in Yunnan and the Xiao Quan Elementary School in Sichuan, whereas other important architectural awards include the Architectural Record "Good Design is Good Business" Award, Chinese Architecture Media Award and WA Award. TAO's works have been recognised and published widely, both in China and internationally: for example, it was selected for "Design Vanguard 2012" by New York's *Architectural Record* magazine. Its works have been exhibited in Beijing, Chengdu, Shenzhen, Mannheim, Vienna and at the MoMA in New York.

WEBSITE
www.t-a-o.cn

RESILIENCE

How can architecture provide an enabling framework that can protect the citizen from the harsh realities of environmental, geographic and other circumstantial conditions? Projects such as the Umubano Primary School, Post-Tsunami Housing, Maria Grazia Cutuli Primary School and Reconstruction of the Nahr El-Bared Refugee Camp demonstrate the necessity of an architecture of resilience capable of accommodating and sheltering their users from the plight of environmental, social and political injustice.

UMUBANO PRIMARY SCHOOL
Kigali, Rwanda

Located almost on the equator in a poor neighbourhood of the Rwandan capital of Kigali, the Umubano Primary School was designed as a self-sustaining organisation that offers quality education at affordable fees, especially for vulnerable or orphaned children. At full capacity it will welcome 300 pupils aged between 5 and 11.

Constructed on a steep hillside, the school comprises seven single-storey buildings that house nine classrooms, an administrative block and a library, laid out over five terraced "platforms" to combat the slope. This ingenious solution, which also helps solve problems of heavy water flow and consequent hill erosion in the rainy seasons, defines classroom space and also "courtyards" or open, shaded teaching areas, as well as separate play areas for different age groups. Each platform accommodates two or three classrooms linked by zigzagging walkways that connect the different levels.

The classrooms are housed in simple rectangular buildings, allowing flexibility in the internal arrangement of furniture, with walls of local earth bricks (left unplastered) topped by double-slope corrugated roof panels supported on a simple steel structure. The "back" walls act as retaining structures since they lie against the slope of the hill. The introduction of a clerestory into the height difference between the two roof pitches provides cross ventilation and natural light. "Holes" created in the walls through a varied placing of the bricks in certain areas also aid natural air circulation (and so, reduced energy consumption), and create interesting patterns of light and shade, enlivening the linearity of the front facades. Ceilings and doors are thatched with reed, a traditional skill; indeed, the use of local materials, skills and workforce meant that the project is well integrated into its site.

Outside, small stone retaining walls form terraced steps that, together with the long low shapes of the brick buildings, make the school instantly recognisable from afar and double as good outdoor seating. Indeed, the school has become a landmark for the neighbourhood, which has benefited greatly from its presence: the government serviced the site with electricity and water; streets and drainage systems were improved; and new settlers were attracted by the opportunity for quality education at low costs, in turn upgrading their houses.

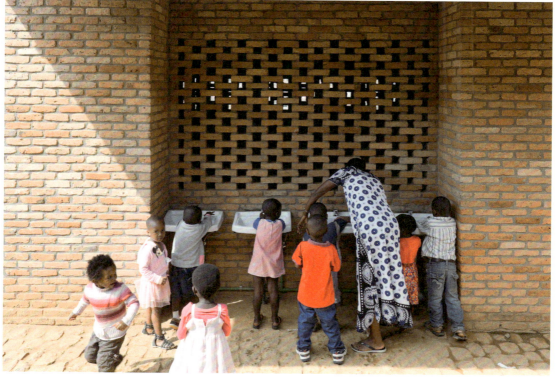

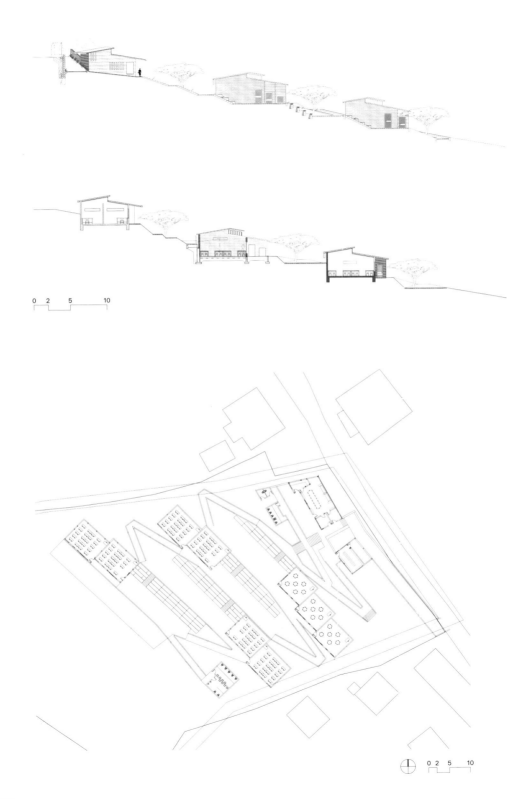

UMUBANO PRIMARY SCHOOL
Kigali, Rwanda

CLIENT
A Partner in Education, London, UK:
Brooks Newark, founder and executive director

ARCHITECT
MASS Design Group, Boston, USA:
Michael P. Murphy Jr, co-founder and executive director
Alan Ricks, co-founder and chief operating officer
Sierra Bainbridge, senior director
Ryan Leidner, Marika Shiori-Clark, Ebbe Straithairn, Branden Collins, Andrew Brose, project team

CONTRACTOR AND ENGINEER
UJENGE, Kigali, Rwanda:
Patrick Setibatigita, principal

PROJECT DATA
Built area: 900 m^2
Cost: 350,000 USD
Commission: January 2007
Design: January 2007
Construction: July 2010–July 2011
Completion: July 2011

MASS DESIGN GROUP
MASS Design Group is a non-profit architectural firm committed to building better buildings, as well as enabling the people who build them. Guided under the leadership of co-founders Michael Murphy and Alan Ricks and director Sierra Bainbridge, MASS has offices in Boston, MA, and Kigali, Rwanda. The firm is currently working in Rwanda, Liberia, Haiti, the Democratic Republic of the Congo and Uganda. MASS employs a mode atypical from traditional architecture, conducting immersive research in communities not only to build context-appropriate, safer and healthier facilities, but also to leverage local material markets, lead training workshops, spur craft development and foster economic empowerment in the process. MASS believes that the inclusive process to construct, maintain, learn from and replicate this new infrastructure is instrumental to healthier and more resilient communities.

WEBSITES
www.apartnerineducation.org
www.massdesigngroup.org

POST-TSUNAMI HOUSING
Kirinda, Sri Lanka

Most of the houses in the predominantly Muslim fishing village of Kirinda on the south-east coast of Sri Lanka were destroyed by the 2004 tsunami, with the consequent temporary relocation of several hundred residents who had lost all means for making their livelihood.

Among several reconstruction projects led by private actors, NGOs and the Sri Lankan government, the businessman Philip Bay launched the Kirinda Trust Fund to raise the necessary funding, and brought in the architect Shigeru Ban (who worked in a voluntary capacity) to design housing, a mosque (completion, late 2015) and a tree plantation for a 15,900-square-metre site in the village, approximately 200 metres from the Indian Ocean and Kirinda Harbour, centre of the local economy.

The project aimed to have new homes ready for the displaced families as rapidly as possible and to maintain the village's pre-disaster social and cultural arrangements. So the same plots were used – although all were now connected to electricity and clean water, and each was provided with a septic tank – and, after consultation with the residents, construction of the 67 houses began in June 2005.

The tropical climate played a significant role in the design: being warm with little seasonal variation and very humid with a monsoon season in the autumn, ventilation was a prime consideration, whereas no heating was required. The detached single-storey, pitched-roof houses comprise a kitchen and bathroom separated from the main living quarters by a central open-roofed courtyard, as stipulated by government norms. Provision is also made in the living area for a more secluded women's space.

Local materials were used throughout: compressed earth blocks for the walls; various woods for the frame, roof trusses and modular, locally prefabricated units for parts of the walls; and clay roofing tiles – consequently distinguishing these houses from the typical local architecture of concrete blocks and corrugated-iron roof sheeting. The central shaded space for family activity, which can be closed off from the areas either side of it by wooden folding doors, facilitates ventilation, and the slatted wooden screens of the upper gable walls ensure a good cross-circulation of air. In addition, the site was planted with more palm trees and indigenous shrubs and an improved drainage system for the three small lakes surrounding the village was implemented.

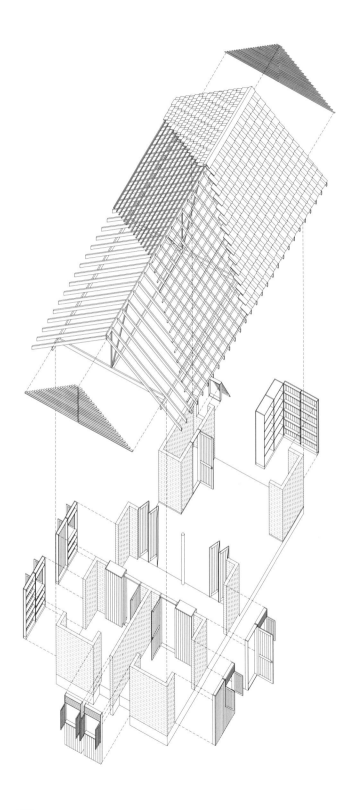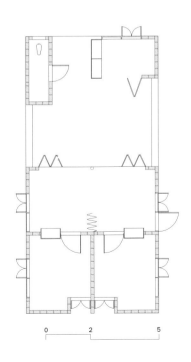

POST-TSUNAMI HOUSING
Kirinda, Sri Lanka

CLIENT
Philip Bay, developer and fundraiser, Washington, USA

ARCHITECT
Shigeru Ban Architects, Tokyo, Japan:
Shigeru Ban, principal
Anthony Benjamin, project manager

LOCAL ARCHITECT
PWA Architects, Colombo, Sri Lanka:
Philip Weeraratne, Sumith Perera, architects

PROJECT COORDINATORS
Pradip Jayawardana, Charith Goonetilleke, Colombo, Sri Lanka

LANDSCAPE ARCHITECT
Shitanee Ivonne Balasunya, Colombo, Sri Lanka

PROJECT DATA
Site area: 3195 m^2
Ground-floor area: 71 m^2 each house
Cost: 1,700,000 USD
Cost per house: 15,000 USD
Commission: December 2004
Design: January 2005
Construction: June 2005
Completion: 2007

SHIGERU BAN
Born in Tokyo in 1957, Shigeru Ban attended the Southern California Institute of Architecture (SCI-Arc) and graduated from the Cooper Union School of Architecture in 1984. In 1985, he established Shigeru Ban Architects, a private practice in Tokyo. In 1995, he began working as a consultant to the United Nations High Commissioner for Refugees and in the same year established an NGO, Voluntary Architects' Network (VAN).
Renowned for his innovative ideas in works such as the Curtain Wall House (Tokyo, Japan, 1995), Japan Pavilion, Expo 2000 (Hanover, Germany), Nomadic Museum (2005, 2006, 2007), Nicolas G. Hayek Centre (Tokyo, Japan, 2007), and Centre Pompidou-Metz (Metz, France, 2010), today, Ban operates three offices, in Tokyo, New York and Paris. He has contributed his knowledge, skills and energy to disaster-relief projects, including the Paper Log House (Kobe, Japan, 1995; Turkey, 2000, India, 2002), Paper Church (Kobe, 1995), Tsunami Reconstruction Project (Kirinda, Sri Lanka, 2005), Temporary Elementary School (Chengdu, China 2008), L'Aquila Temporary Concert Hall (L'Aquila, Italy, in progress), and waterproof shelters currently underway in Haiti.
Ban has been awarded a number of prizes, including the Grande Médaille d'Or de l'Académie d'Architecture, France (2004), Arnold W. Brunner Memorial Prize in Architecture (2005), Thomas Jefferson Foundation Medal in Architecture (2005), L'Ordre National du Mérite, France (2009), and L'Ordre des Arts et des Lettres, France (2010). He served on the jury for the Pritzker Architecture Prize from 2007 to 2009. He was a Professor at Keio University, Japan, from 2001 to 2008 and is a Visiting Professor at Harvard University Graduate School of Design and a Visiting Critic at Cornell University (2010).

WEBSITE
www.shigerubanarchitects.com

MARIA GRAZIA CUTULI PRIMARY SCHOOL
Khushrud Village, Herat, Afghanistan

The school was built to commemorate the Italian journalist Maria Grazia Cutuli, who was killed in 2001 when her convoy was ambushed during the US-Taliban war. The design was commissioned in 2009 from four Italian architectural offices by the Maria Grazia Cutuli Foundation with the aim of supporting programmes in the fields of education and social promotion for children and women in countries like Afghanistan. The site of Khushrud – some 12 kilometres from Herat City – was selected and 6000 square metres of land for a school was donated by the village. A local construction company started building in June 2010 with the head of the village providing skilled and unskilled labour, and the first students began lessons in April 2011.

The very distinctive, cobalt blue school tucked inside its walled compound stands on the edge of the village in stark contrast to the surrounding wide-open, flat plains of vineyards and agricultural fields, with mountains in the distance to the north. Its layout of one-storey blocks alternating with intervening green spaces might recall Herat's traditional cluster-based villages, though the architects stress their search for an innovative educational space, and the outside spaces were specifically designed as a "green classroom". To this end, the external spaces of courtyards and walkways were interspersed with raised, irregularly shaped, cultivated beds, and trees were planted.

The eight classrooms and administration block at the entrance are linked by corridors, which also give access from every room to the gardens outside, and the whole complex is dominated by the double-height library, which stands out above the enclosing walls as a landmark from afar. With a large, bright, ground-floor area, the library was also designed as a meeting space for the community, and its decorative glass-block openings in the upper level of the brickwork recall Herati pigeon towers to a certain extent. The reinforced-concrete frames of the blocks are clad in brick from the local brickworks, but there is little other reference to Herat's rich heritage of traditional brick architecture. The vivid blues covering all the exterior walls are also most unusual for this context.

Initially planned for an estimated 240 pupils, the school now works at more than full capacity with 400 girls attending in the mornings and 400 boys in the afternoons.

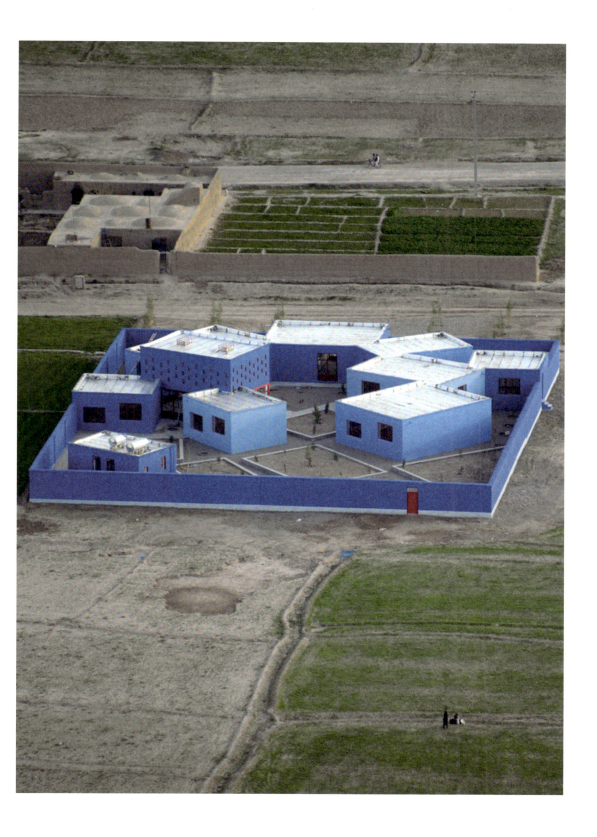

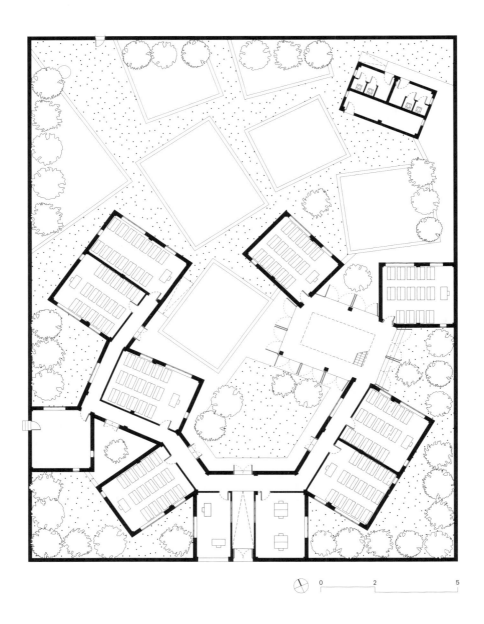

MARIA GRAZIA CUTULI PRIMARY SCHOOL
Khushrud Village, Herat, Afghanistan

CLIENT
Maria Grazia Cutuli Foundation, Rome, Italy

ARCHITECTS
2A+P/A, Rome, Italy:
Gianfranco Bombaci, Matteo Costanzo, architects
Valeria Bartolacci, Antonino Crea, Domenica Fiorini, Maxim Mangold, Valentina Morelli, Consuelo Nunez Ciuffa, project team

Mario Cutuli, Rome, Italy

IaN+, Rome, Italy:
Carmelo Baglivo, Luca Galofaro, Stefania Manna, architects
Juliette Dubroca, Simone Lapenta, project team

ma0/emmeazero, Rome, Italy:
Massimo Ciuffini, Ketty Di Tardo, Alberto Iacovoni, Luca La Torre, architects
Manfredi Mazziotta, Marco Bordone, project team

STRUCTURAL AND SERVICE ENGINEER
Studio Croci Associati, Rome, Italy:
Federico Croci, principal

LANDSCAPE CONSULTANT
Gruppo di Volontariato Civile (GVC), Bologna, Italy:
Luigi Politani

SITE SUPERVISOR
Ali Reza Taheri, Herat, Afghanistan

CONTRACTOR
Behsazan Sharq Building & Construction Co., Herat, Afghanistan

KHUSHRUD VILLAGE LEADER AND SUBCONTRACTOR
Jamal Shah Ahmadi, Khushrud, Afghanistan

PROJECT DATA
Site area: 2000 m^2
Ground-floor area: 650 m^2
Cost: 189,000 USD
Commission: May 2009
Design: March 2010–June 2010
Construction: June 2010–April 2011
Completion: April 2011

2A+P/A
2A+P/A is an architectural office established by Gianfranco Bombaci and Matteo Costanzo, based in Rome. The architects of 2A+P/A have publicly presented their projects at, and realised site-specific installations for, several international exhibitions, such as the NAI in Rotterdam, the 11th Venice Architecture Biennale, and Expo 2010 in Shanghai. Their work was also showcased in a solo exhibition in Rome entitled "The Pop Out Show".

MARIO CUTULI
Mario Cutuli lives and works in Rome, where he graduated in architecture in 1994. He opened his own studio in 1996. From 2001 to 2007, he worked on urban and land policy on the staff of the office of the mayor of Rome, Walter Veltroni; from 2007 to 2008, he collaborated with the architect Massimiliano Fuksas as coordinator for art direction in the EUR New Convention Centre in Rome; from 2008 to 2010, he worked as a public transport consultant. From 2007 to 2012 he was president of the Maria Grazia Cutuli Foundation.

IAN+
IaN+ is a multidisciplinary agency that aims for the place where theory and practice of architecture overlap and meet. In 2006, the studio won the Italian Architecture Gold Medal for its first completed work and, in 2010, it was selected for the Iakov Chernikhov Prize. Currently IaN+ is involved in the construction of a public swimming pool in Rome, two buildings for the "Ospedale del Mare" in Naples, and a housing project in Taiwan.

MA0/EMMEAZERO
ma0/emmeazero has been active since 1996 and has designed and completed many projects for buildings and public spaces. Its work has been published in *Detail*, *Domus*, *Abitare* and other important journals.

WEBSITES
www.2ap.it/en/home.html
www.ianplus.it
www.ma0.it

RECONSTRUCTION OF NAHR EL-BARED REFUGEE CAMP
Akkar, Lebanon

This is a post-war reconstruction project involving the rebuilding of Nahr el-Bared Refugee Camp after it was destroyed during the 2007 war that led to the displacement of 26,000 individuals (5000 families). Founded during the Arab-Israeli conflict of 1948, it is the oldest and largest Palestinian refugee camp in Lebanon and is located 16 kilometres north of the city of Tripoli on the shores of the Mediterranean.

The primary aim behind the reconstruction was to preserve the Camp's pre-destruction neighbourhood layout and social fabric, augmented by an improved urban environment (common area upgrading and infrastructure) and living conditions (proper ventilation and open space). To these ends, a community-based grassroots committee from within the Camp drafted a set of principles and guidelines stating the community's vision for reconstruction and initiated a massive asset-mapping operation; large-scale, walk-in maps were made to help residents indicate the precise locations of their houses, the neighbourhoods, landmarks, schools and so on, and these became a master plan for reconstruction.

In 2008, the work, divided into eight geographical construction phases, was begun by the United Nations Relief and Works Agency (UNRWA), with about 80% of the labour force Palestinian, aiding socio-economic recovery in the Camp. To make more public open space available and to increase natural light and ventilation, the footprint of buildings was reduced, but this deduction in plot area was made up for vertically in increased building height, up to a maximum of four storeys. Roads have been widened, pedestrian routes improved, open courts introduced and, most importantly, infrastructure networks laid – for water supply, storm water, sewage, electricity and tele-communications. Two layout options have been designed for each apartment type and roof terraces have been reintroduced to provide private outdoor space and views of the sea, as well as to house water tanks. Buildings are made of cast-in-place reinforced-concrete columns, steel beams, slabs and CMU blocks for the walls. Adjacent walls are set with a 5-centimetre air space between, thus aiding insulation as well as possible future expansion vertically as families increase in size but desire to remain in one building.

The phased construction approach means that displaced people can return as soon as their new homes are ready, while lessons learned in early phases can be incorporated in later ones: the first families returned in 2011.

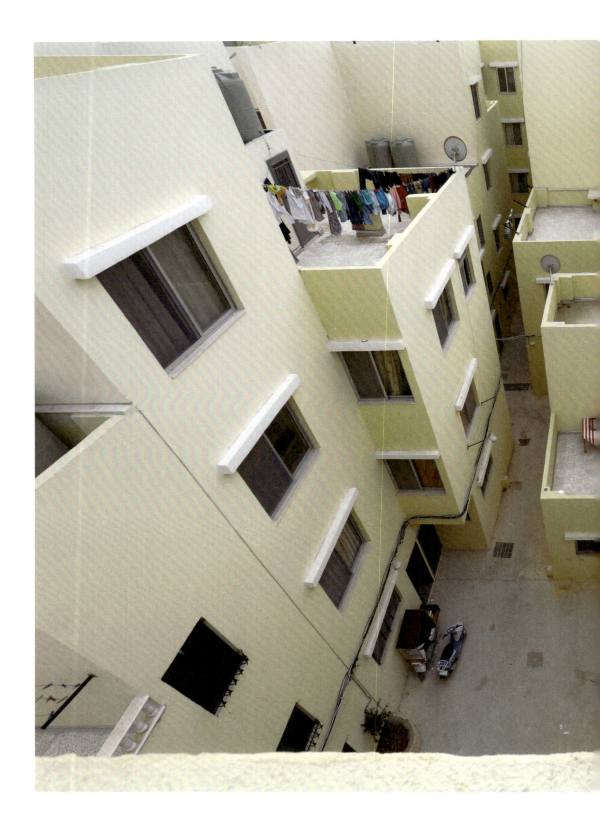

RECONSTRUCTION OF NAHR EL-BARED REFUGEE CAMP
Akkar, Lebanon

CLIENTS
United Nations Relief and Works Agency for Palestine Refugees in the Near East (UNRWA), Lebanon Field Office, Beirut, Lebanon

Refugees of Nahr el-Bared Camp, Lebanon

ARCHITECT PLANNERS
UNRWA, Beirut, Lebanon:
Muna Budeiri, architect planner, deputy director and head of Camp Improvement Unit
Aditya Kumar, Abdel Nasser El-Ayyi, Hala Al Asir, Ghassan Ghafoor, Rana Hassan, Hanane Yazigi, Adeil Bahloul, Mohamad Maw'id, Jamal Al Dali

Nahr el-Bared Reconstruction Commission for Civil Action and Studies (NBRC), Akkar, Lebanon:
Ismail Cheikh Hassan, architect planner, co-founder
Jamal Friejeh, Fathi Rabih, Ahmad Ma'ari Hussam Cha'ban, Raidah Wehbeh, Samah Badr, Mahasin Mahmoud, Imtiaaz Loubani, Hasan Mawid

OTHER CONTRIBUTORS:
UNRWA Northern Management Unit, Beirut, Lebanon:
Rim Sabalbal, Jenan Diab, Jihad Farah, Patrizio Jellici, Marie-Josee Anjoul, Saba Innab, Lyne Jabri, Nada Sabbagh, Rim Sabouneh, Yasmine Lutfi El-Haj Ahmed, Maen Alzaher, Nibal Abdulrazzak, Hanan Suleiman, Majdi Zeid, Mahmoud Ahmad, Abdel Karim Meri, Alia Hamdan, Loai Tannous, Nadine el-Marouk, Hussam el-Jazzar, Mahmoud al-Ghadban, Daoud Korman, Nidal Ayyoub, Sebastian May, Charles Higgins, Mohammed Abdel A'al

UNRWA Lebanon Field Office, Beirut, Lebanon:
Richard Cook, Salvatore Lombardo, Roger Davies

UNRWA Headquarters, Amman, Jordan:
Filippo Grandi, Karen Konning, Issam Miqdadi, Rafiq al Abed, Akram Abuamira, Salah Ismail, Ali Alsayyed, Nauman Abu Hammad

NBRC, Akkar, Lebanon:
Kamleh el Wannas, Tayseer el Sayid, Ahmad Waked, Ahmad Nimr, Ibrahim Hamid, Hasan Mihyi el Deen Abu Ali, Imad Oudeh, Zeidan Wehbeh, Najib Oudeh, Khaled Maw'id, Rabih Salah, Racha Najdi, Marwan Ghandour, Habib Debs, Mona Fawaz, Imad Bashir, Maher Abu Samra, Amro Saedidine, Najwa Doghman, Nadine Bekdache, Muzna Masri
Salim Al-khazen, consultant

LPHU Lebanese Handicapped Union, Beirut, Lebanon

OTHER PARTNERS:
Government of Lebanon, Lebanese Palestinian Dialogue Committee, Beirut Lebanon

PROJECT DATA
Site area: 196,300 m^2
Cost: 171,150,000 USD
Commission: July 2007
Design: July 2008–ongoing
Construction: December 2009–ongoing
Completion: April 2011–ongoing

UNRWA
UNRWA provides assistance, protection and advocacy for some five million registered Palestine refugees. UNRWA's human development and humanitarian services encompass primary and vocational education, primary health care, a social safety net, community support, infrastructure and camp improvement, microfinance and emergency response, including in situations of armed conflict.

NBRC
NBRC is a local community grassroots initiative that was launched by predominantly local professionals and activists in 2007 during the destruction of Nahr el-Bared. Its main aim was to develop local consensus, studies and designs for the Camp's reconstruction, while opposing top-down planning for its post-war reconstruction. After the master plan was approved and the reconstruction initiated, the NBRC was disbanded by 2011.

WEBSITE
www.unrwa.org/index.php

ON LANDSCAPE
Michel Desvigne

The projects that we have considered for the Aga Khan Award for Architecture were sometimes related to extreme situations of crisis or impoverishment, which, I think, raise new issues. I was touched to see that these projects' procedures – their transformation processes – were close to those I practice. Obviously, their intensity, their urgency, gives them an exceptional character. The Jury's choices gradually moved towards projects based upon process, rather than objects (even though these were sometimes spectacular). This obviously relates to the particularities of the Aga Khan Award for Architecture, but probably also marks a turning point in history. A sense of seriousness, a desire for authenticity and legitimacy dominates. Thus, all the awarded projects are deep-rooted in a specific social and cultural context, and have a strong and readable consistency. Critical debates have focused on these specific values that belong to the essence of architecture. Many of the topics we discussed are contemporary landscape issues, and I would like to put these issues into perspective here.

A large number of cities are adopting territorial projects and visions. These projects anticipate the future and extend beyond any administrative limits, often merging with those of natural geography. I believe this is something more than a simple momentary preoccupation. In some countries (for example France), a deficit of projects is giving way to planning on a large scale and sometimes over long periods. Everything suggests that a lack of financial resources is discouraging the production of icons in favour of territorial, collective and sustainable projects. The desire to construct is shifting its focus from the spectacular object towards more modest prototypes of territorial schemes. These modest but heartening undertakings give me a sense of optimism.

These preconditions, sometimes considered temporary and often drawn up with the urgency imposed by an impending election, are conceived with a sort of detachment. Paradoxically, such precarious conditions can result in lasting works of architecture, since they are detached from any notion of statecraft and above all their modesty allows for any kind of future transformation. It is in this sense that they can last. I believe in the potential of the recomposition of the geography of our urban territories. I believe in the creation of public spaces that are lacking at the scale of the major urban expansions. An urban culture on a large scale is taking shape. I am delighted about this situation, in which society seems ready to tackle the transformation of its territories.

Several of our projects of territorial recomposition have prompted us to re-examine the park system that had been initiated by Frederick Law Olmsted in the United States in the 19th century. This system is founded on a rigorous identification of geographical structures: a river in Boston, former stream beds turned into open sewers in Washington DC. Olmsted's work consisted in amplifying the presence of these natural elements – plentiful planting on the reliefs, water management, installation of infrastructure, traffic routes – in ways that would create robust foundations for the development of the city. Some of the park systems conceived in this way, such as the one in Boston, remain legible and still preserve all their meaning today. If this set of parks forms a coherent and intelligent whole, it is because it is based on a natural geography, on a very large scale. In the city, this geography is completed, transposed by artificial elements. These elements are minor on the geographical scale, which preserves its coherence, but are immense on the scale of Boston's new districts, giving them structure. Thus, looking at the landscape of the 19th century, it does not seem illusory to me to propose "amplified" modes of management of landscape, within a period of time of about 50 years, in order to provide a geographical anchorage for fragmented urban territories.

The territories on which we – landscape architects and city planners – are called to act pose multiple and complex problems, sometimes on a very large scale. Hence, we experience difficulty in seeing, understanding, measuring and arbitrating. Perceiving urban phenomena of large dimensions is, in fact, arduous. Everyone creates their own mental image, an abstraction that obscures the reality. Thus the maps of a large territory are rarely the expression of a physical reality. Which city in what territory? What kind of boundaries? What is being measured? These are similar questions to those that scientists ask on a cellular scale. Comparing our approach to some of their works, concerning equally complex phenomena, makes us aware of our fragility and of the risk of becoming content with symbolic, ideological, even commercial approaches, as well as our distance from real environmental problems. Perceiving the scale and having the right response at the right dimension is, in my view, the key to the success of a recomposition of a territory.

In methodological terms, a permanent gauging is needed, like the systematic adjustments made on old reflex cameras before taking a picture. Gauging obliges us to tackle all scales at once: implementing a strategy of organisation over the long term, looking at things on smaller scales (of the order of 250 hectares) for places in which pieces of city are actually going to be built, and carrying out concrete experiments on even smaller scales (10 or so hectares). This simultaneity of work on varying scales forces us to keep adjusting our gaze so that each new point of view explains or questions the previous one, and permits the evaluation of hypotheses formulated for future development.

Adjusting the gaze and evaluating the intervention are indispensable for avoiding fixed notions of development of territories that are prevalent today. In fact, this is the basis of the first phase of many projects that are constructed around the globe without due acknowledgement or awareness of their future development. I have finally ended up with a picture of contemporary city planning as the addition of the "first phases" of developments that will never exist, and that may constitute conceptual errors.
In order to remedy this, it is our job and our duty to conceive intelligent "wholes", while giving them constants, intangible and lasting elements with which it is possible to work on the transformation of territories.

Many projects recognised by the Award contribute to the transformation of cities and territories that have already been greatly modified and rendered artificial. This is particularly so as a consequence of addressing built environments dating from the second half of the 20th century. During the 20th century, many cities were developed without any awareness of the totality of the building mass and without creating public spaces on a par with the scale of the urbanisation produced.

Now it is a question of repairing, transforming and reinstating spaces and territories that are already inhabited and occupied. The urgent need is to get the proportion between landscape and built-up areas into balance again. History teaches us that 30% of a balanced territory is open space, a ratio whose legitimacy it is difficult to get developers to accept today. So every city proceeds by successive repairs or small additions – a series of projects of transformation that are carried out over a long period. Around 30 years is needed to create a new district. Over such a long timescale, the landscape is transformed through layers. It is not the fixed anticipation of a project. Each layer is new and transforms the previous one.

Returning to an earlier layer, one finds that things did not go according to plan, no more so in a park than in an urban context. Fortunately, the master plan is never translated into reality in the way that was intended. So our view of our first physical interventions has to be modified. It is necessary to select, to create a hierarchy. The first layer is decisive, but leaves room for numerous possibilities, adaptations and adjustments. Subjected to a process of this kind, these places may seem unfinished. This idea of incompleteness may pertain to a desire for coherence, the desire to transform territories in step with what is constructed, with the practices that are adopted. Incompleteness also allows you to remain open to developments and to differentiated appropriations. So I consider these spaces subject to successive transformations as "intermediate natures", flexible ones, capable of playing on duration and temporality.

Being a landscape architect means contributing to the building of a common territory. A public space in an urban centre is undoubtedly the most visible of these common heritages, the one that bestows identity on a district or a city. In European cities, public spaces assume configurations that are always specific and put up stiff resistance to standardisation and globalisation.

Some of the projects reviewed (especially the Altach Islamic Cemetery, Austria, by Bernardo Bader, and the Rabat-Salé Urban Infrastructure Project, Morocco, by Marc Mimram) were very close to landscape projects – not gardens as such, but similar to territorial approaches. This gives me much pleasure, especially as I understand that the Aga Khan Award for Architecture will take an ever-increasing interest in these approaches.

TURKISH ARCHITECTURE TODAY!

Hashim Sarkis is the Aga Khan Professor of Landscape Architecture and Urbanism in Muslim Societies and Director of the Aga Khan Program at the Graduate School of Design at Harvard University, where he teaches design studios on architecture, infrastructure and public space. His recent research interest has focused on the significant changes that have taken place in the urban environment in Turkey and he is the editor of *A Turkish Triangle: Ankara, Istanbul, and Izmir at the Gates of Europe*, a study of the roles of these three urban poles over the last 20 years.

In a conversation with two prominent Turkish architects, **Han Tümertekin**, member of the Steering Committee since 2008, and **Murat Tabanlıoğlu**, member of the 2013 Master Jury, Sarkis points to the significant changes that have occurred within Turkey recently and the architects explore them and try to put them into perspective.

The Turkish construction company has become the new paradigm of efficiency, scale and reliability in the construction sector of the Middle East and Central Asia. After the soap opera, it is perhaps one of the best known of Turkish exports. Over the past 15 years, these giant companies have become gargantuan, growing both horizontally, to buy out their competitors, and vertically, to include real estate, design and the building industry. They have also generated major exchanges in terms of building and development culture for Turkish engineers. How has this affected Turkish architecture? Have these skills been developed within Turkey and then exported? Are issues of the scale of development reflective of this capacity to build big?

Turkey has gone through a boom period during which construction has been a major signifier, even the leading sector of the economy. The increasing rate of urbanisation in Turkey during the 1950s led to a huge shortage of housing and consequently to uncontrolled development, especially in the form of squatter zones. The housing projects of Emlak Kredi Bank, a state agency aiming to control housing development by providing long-term, low-interest loans to middle-class families, especially for housing construction, include projects such as Istanbul Ataköy (sections I–II, 1957–62 and 1959–64), a new suburb on the outskirts of the city that reflects the political and economic situation of the period. This was a modernist urban-planning exercise, but, in the following years, and as a result of radical shifts in both Turkish politics, society and culture and the government's aim to integrate with global markets, such projects increasingly took the form of gated communities or residential

Ipekyol Textile Factory, Edirne, 2006 (2010 Award recipient)

high-rises in suburbs throughout Turkey, such as the Bahçeşehir and Ataşehir communities in Istanbul. TOKI (the Housing Development Administration) has since gained considerable power in the construction sector.

Starting in the 1980s, the beginning of the period of liberalisation and privatisation in Turkey, thanks to Turgut Özal's policies, huge investments were made in the build-operate-transfer model. Hayati Tabanlıoğlu's Ataköy Tourism Complex is one of the leading examples, including the first shopping mall, Galleria (1986). In the meantime, construction also became a good business investment for previously industrial sector investors or textile producers. The preferred investment was tourism on the Mediterranean coast, Antalya being the favoured location. The shore was filled with clusters of hotel buildings while no plans at all were drawn up for the hinterland. Due to this practice, there is an increasing emphasis on matters relating to fashion linked to this particular type of built environment. The weekend papers abound with advertisements, marketing a "life style" of new luxury residential towers with shopping, sports and recreational facilities.

Following the competitions for several new international airports, launched by Turkey's General Directorate of State Airports Authority in the 1990s, the build-operate-transfer model was applied to several airports (Istanbul, Ankara, Izmir, Bodrum, Dalaman) after 2000. One of the main reasons for privatisation was the need to invest in terminals, since passenger numbers have increased dramatically in the last decade and terminal facilities were inadequate and the source of great congestion. By utilising the build-operate-transfer model the state was able to shift the burden of financing and operating to the private sector. Many contractors also became operators. The operating period granted for build-operate-transfer contracts varied significantly, depending on the income that could be generated from the operations against the cost of the terminal construction.

In the last two decades, Turkish contractors have acquired the "skill" of building big and fast. Benefiting national practice, Turkish construction firms have applied their experience worldwide, mainly in the CIS countries and MENA. Turkish architects designing projects overseas can count on the efficiency and reliability of these firms to get their designs built. In countries such as Turkmenistan and Kazakhstan, the presidents are directly involved in construction projects. In the case of Astana, a master plan was developed by Kisho Kurokawa at the behest of President Nazarbayev, and then world-renowned architects were invited to take part in competitions proposing significant buildings for the newly established capital. Turkish architects and contractors also worked on many other projects in the region. As in the Kazakhstan example, several Turkish contractors have worked efficiently with international and Turkish architects all around the world, having already proven their practicality, enforceability, adaptability, speed of construction capacity and reliability to international investors.

The current government has taken the role of the state as developer to higher levels, particularly with the instrument of TOKI (the Housing Development Administration) and its siblings. This controversial tool and its consequences are being monitored by financial and housing experts. TOKI towns have undoubtedly drawn major criticism from the architectural and urban design world as well. Beyond the immediate and obvious criticisms, could you reflect on the impact that TOKI has had on the architectural make up of cities in Turkey and on the means by which the profession has been responding to this phenomenon.

TOKI has been operating directly under the Prime Ministry since 2003 and is said to have contracted more than 420,000 housing units. According to TOKI sources, the stated level of activity of the agency corresponds to an investment spending of approximately $35 billion, the equivalent of "20 new cities, with 100,000 population each" (2010 data). TOKI builds on the outskirts of cities, regardless of the "place" and actual needs; indeed, the results are all similar high-rise apartment buildings, encouraging spread-out, car-dependent living – human depots – despite the fact that TOKI aims primarily to contribute to earthquake-resistant infrastructure in a healthy urban environment, granting equal rights for housing for all. Very recently, and departing from a line of projects with no thought for good design or planning, nor even the employment of architects, TOKI is now launching architectural competitions. And, although rare, good examples, like the Bio Istanbul project, are underway. It may be an auspicious omen that the recently established Ministry of Environment and City Planning is headed by Erdoğan Bayraktar, former TOKI chairman. The most recent and excellent news is that master planning will be enforced before the start of all urban renovation projects in derelict zones and regions at the risk of earthquakes.

The government's large-scale urban renewal projects, meant to complement the centennial celebrations of the Turkish Republic in 2023, have been cautiously received by urban planners, architects and the general public. Indeed, three of these "magnificent" projects are controversial: namely the "Second Strait", the third bridge over the Bosphorus and the airport to the north of Istanbul.

Furthermore, the lack of any impact evaluation is one of the worst aspects of TOKI policies. TOKI's impact on the economy and urban landscape should be evaluated carefully. If we have a better understanding of TOKI and its impact, we will have a better understanding of the Turkish economy and social policies in general.

The current design scene in Istanbul has caught the world's attention. There is a growing design consciousness among the younger generation. Once again, Turkish industry has played a major role in channelling its production and products to the building industry. As architects, you have worked closely with the design industries of Turkey and you have tried to innovate through them and with them. Has this industry been responsive to the demands of the new generation of designers in Turkey?

In the 1960s, when the Atatürk Cultural Centre was first built, its aluminium lattice facade had to be made in Germany because the building industry in Turkey was not capable of providing it. In 1969, the building burnt down but was rebuilt and reopened in 1977. This time the facade was produced locally by Arçelik, a leading producer of household appliances and electronics in Turkey.

During the last decade, Turkish labour and production have enabled the Turkish building materials sector to compete throughout the world. Local productions respond to international associations' choices and uses of contemporary materials. Moreover, competent local labour makes "tailor-made" production possible, thus sustaining the design and building industry. For example, the steel infrastructure for a building in Astana is now produced in Ankara and transported to Kazakhstan, together with all the sanitary ware and furniture. Unique mesh applications and glassware produced in Turkey is compatible with world standards, as the industry is highly responsive to new design requirements; these are designed by architects as one-off pieces and the prototypes are manufactured and applied accordingly. It is also very common for architects to collaborate with furniture manufacturers. For example, during the construction of a project in Istanbul, Paşabahçe Glass Industry and

Trade Inc. (first established in 1935), new products were designed based on the specifications provided by the designer and these new materials have become a regular product in the company's line since then.

In terms of Turkish natural stone and marble, the efforts of associations like the Building Material Producers Association (IMSAD) and Istanbul Mineral Exporters' Association (IMIB) have brought Turkish products onto the international market. Turkey has one of the world's richest marble deposits with more than 400 different colours, textures and patterns of natural stones.

In recalling its unique ancient value, the Iznik tile is versatile in design and is also adaptable to clients' demands. It is both an ancient and contemporary Turkish material. Today, ceramic manufacture is one of the strongest and most competitive products in the Turkish building material industry.

Architectural education has not always adequately reflected the demands or conditions of the development and building culture. Sometimes schools of architecture play the role of professional training outlets and at others they become sites of withdrawal and criticism, or of production of alternatives. How would you describe the scene in Turkey today, particularly bearing in mind the large number of new schools of architecture that have been created in the past decade.

Besides the established state universities such as Middle East Technical University (one of the top 60 on the world list), Istanbul Technical University and Yıldız Technical University, many private and foundation universities that opened during the last 10 years include architecture in their programmes. Founding a university is considered a prestigious investment for a business person and it is usually also facilitated by the state, especially through land donation. Out of many, the credible ones have distinguished themselves by the quality and performance of their graduates.

Istanbul's Bilgi University is one such example, distinguishing itself with a graduate design programme. Founded by Professor İhsan Bilgin in 2005, this graduate programme includes leading professors from the state universities among its faculty. Importantly, Bilgi University provides students with the opportunity to pursue their studies in a high-intensity studio environment guided by practicing architects, such as Han Tümertekin, Murat Tabanlıoğlu, Can Çinici, Emre Arolat, Arif Suyabatmaz, Mehmet Kütükçüoğlu, Nevzat Sayın and Cem Çelik.

An interdisciplinary education with international standards in the field of architecture aims to guide students towards a more liberal, creative and innovative product and design, and teach them to use and invent diverse tools and techniques.

B2 House, Ayvacik, 2001 (2004 Award recipient)

The Aga Khan Award for Architecture has engaged with Turkish architects and architecture from the beginning and has responded (rather rewardingly) to the different experiments in Turkish architecture over the past three decades, while also awarding other attempts at experimentation and reinventing regional types and national styles. However, it is not until the last three cycles that projects that have distanced themselves from investing in conscious iconographies have made it to the foreground. Could you high-light the impact that the Award has had on the Turkish design scene, the messages it sends in terms of valuation, and whether, in the midst of the recent wave of the Turkish construction boom, some quality can be extracted from the sheer quantity being produced.

In the first cycle of the Aga Khan Award for Architecture in 1980, three projects from Turkey were amongst the winners, two by Turgut Cansever, one of the most prominent architects of his time. In 1983, the Award ceremony took place in Istanbul and when it was announced that Nail Çakirhan, a poet and a journalist who had built a series of summer houses using traditional techniques with the aid of two local carpenters, had been awarded a prize for the only Turkish project selected, the local architectural community was much surprised and a debate about the role of architects ensued. Since then, the works of many prominent Turkish architects have been premiated – Sedad H. Eldem, Behruz Çinici, Sedat Gürel, Cengiz Bektas – with the Award for Han Tümertekin's B2 House (2004) being a milestone, standing out as a good and representative sample

Atatürk Cultural Centre, Istanbul, 1977

of contemporary Turkish architecture. A balance has been achieved between consciously national styles and projects that have pursued different iconographies. The judging body now recognises the progress and capacity of Turkish architects, and, in particular, the work of young architects in Turkey worthy of notice.

The confrontation between historical preservation and urban regeneration has become headline news recently through the Gezi Park demonstrations in Istanbul. It may be very difficult at this moment to bracket off the political and social implications of this confrontation but could you reflect on the role that architects have played in reconciling these two tendencies.

"Now" is the crucial link between past and future. Architecture should claim the "now", linking the other two. In the Gezi Park issue, the past is also now, because the park is still used intensively, and has been since 1943, by many people.

As part of the republican urban development plans for Istanbul, the French urban planner Henri Prost was commissioned in 1939 to produce a master plan. A larger landscaped area was intended to provide a green promenade, leading to Gezi Park, consisting of about 30 hectares of open green space between the zones of Taksim, Nişantaşı and Maçka, including the Dolmabahçe Valley, but this plan was never entirely carried out. In later years, the Park was further eaten into by the construction of hotels around it. However,

Atatürk Cultural Centre in June 2013

even though it is now one of the smallest parks in Istanbul, Gezi Park is a very valuable and much used area in the heart the city.

Today there is a proposal to erase the current use of the Park and replace it with an obsolete icon of the military barracks, built in 1806 and demolished in 1940. There are no physical remains of these barracks, only a story and a few pictures. This is not what the public would like at all but it is being enforced by the city administration. No clear plans have been drawn up for a larger urban study, only rough renderings of the replica of the military barracks.

Taksim Square is framed by Gezi Park on one side and by another landmark on the other, namely the Atatürk Cultural Centre (the AKM). This multi-use cultural centre and opera house was built in the 1960s to a design by Hayati Tabanlıoğlu. Like the square, Atatürk Cultural Centre is a 20th-century project, an example of modern architecture; together, Gezi Park, the AKM and Taksim Square represent different phases and aspects of the Republic of Turkey's vision of those years and its new civil society.

Atatürk Cultural Centre is one of the most important architectural and cultural landmarks in Turkey. The modernist structure has housed Istanbul's state orchestra, opera and ballet since it first opened in 1969. It has also been at the centre of a major controversy ever since the government announced plans to demolish the building and erect a more contemporary complex.

Besides being a listed building, the Cultural Centre is part of the city's socio-cultural heritage. Like every building, it needs renovation and, as a public building serving the citizens via arts and culture, it should be updated from the 20th to the 21st century with new infrastructure, contemporary materials and a functional reorganisation, although such an upgrade should, of course, remain faithful to its original design.

The growth in size of the design "projects" has in many cases entailed the inclusion of urban designers and landscape architects in the team of consultants. This has invariably led to importing these skills from outside Turkey with very mixed results. It may be too early to tell, but could you describe the interactions with such experts and the impact that this kind of import has had on Turkish cities and landscapes.

Istanbul has been rather isolated from the international architectural scene since the days of Bruno Taut in the 1930s and Gordon Bunshaft's Hilton Hotel in the 1950s. However, more recently, with Suha Özkan's involvement, and benefiting from the advantage of having an architect-mayor together with renewed interest in architecture following the 2005 UIA Congress in Istanbul, international competitions are now being held in the city at various scales.

For example, in 2006, Istanbul Municipality selected Zaha Hadid for a public recreational development project for the Kartal district (the Anatolian side of Istanbul) while Ken Yeang was awarded another large urban transformation project for the Küçükçekmece district (the European side of the city). Jury members were Suha Özkan, Hüseyin Kaptan, Michael Sorkin, Sumet Jumsai, Elías Torres Tur and Necati İnceoğlu. Neither of these projects have been realised yet, but the competitions and the emerging concepts have motivated a trend for bettering the city.

Neighbouring Zaha Hadid's Kartal master-plan zone, a competition for the Maltepe-Dragos Industrial Zone Urban Design Project was launched in 2008, with the involvement of a public initiative composed of landowners. The project made a strong comment on the rehabilitation of the landscape.

Similarly, in 2011, the Cendere Valley Urban Development Project organised an architectural competition with the aim of reviving the region and re-establishing its historical credit as a green and lively valley. The idea was supported by the revitalisation of the Kağıthane River, which would engender a natural living environment within the city centre.

As a rare example, since it is a private investor, Zorlu Holding launched an international competition, again under the leadership of Suha Özkan. One hundred and seventeen offices submitted projects for the Zorlu Centre Architecture and Urban Design Competition, which began in June 2007 and was concluded in 2008. Thirteen international offices were then invited to participate in the second stage. After the final evaluation, the projects by Tabanlıoğlu and EAA were selected as joint winners and their combined project was then developed and will be completed by the end of 2013. For the competition, Tabanlıoğlu Architects consulted the landscape designers Martha Schwarz Partners and Craft:Pegg, who designed hard and soft landscape compositions that interlace with the landscape-roof, which in turn acts both as public space, an urban terrace opening out to the Bosphorus, and as a basis for the construction of the Centre, creating an extension of Istanbul's green and urban fabric.

In 2012, the city organised an international competition around the Yenikapi Transfer Point and Archaeopark Area. During the excavations for the transportation projects, the remains of the 1600-year-old "Theodosius Port", together with the remains of "35 antique ships" from the world's largest fleet and more than 10,000 archaeological finds were unearthed; 8500-year-old settlements of the first Neolithic Age were also found in the same excavation area. As a result, the landscape, together with an open-air museum concept, became the core of the project. However, no clear decision has yet been made about the results of this competition.

REDEFINING THE BUILT PROJECT
Mohammad al-Asad

Let us begin with a basic and simple overview. To realise a built project, three parties usually need to be involved: the project owner, designer and builder. They may be fully independent from each other, or may overlap and interconnect significantly. These parties may come together to create simple structures, or highly complex ones involving a large number of players representing multiple skill sets that require sophisticated levels of coordination.

At one end of the spectrum, a project may consist of a simple structure such as a small residence. Its owner is often an individual who hires a builder to both provide its design and to construct it. The builder would construct the project with the aid of a small construction crew.

At the other end of the spectrum are large-scale projects such as a multi-use development of an urban district, an airport or a shopping centre. One party may come up with the idea and another may secure the funding for it. Teams of professionals, including architects and engineers, as well as legal, environmental and real-estate development specialists, among others, would be involved in determining its design. A large and diverse set of construction teams would be responsible for building it.

These simple – and possibly simplistic – preliminary comments have come to apply to the building process all over the world, in both emerging and advanced economies, though with varying levels of sophistication. The increased globalisation that has affected the financing, design and construction of building projects over the past two decades, however, is having a homogenising impact on how such projects are being conceived and implemented everywhere.

A major problem that primarily affects built projects in the developing world, however, is that this general arrangement through which such projects are realised is fully disbanded the moment the project is completed, and the project is more or less left on its own after that. Maintenance and upkeep are barely provided. Additions and modifications – and these will inevitably take place – are made to the project in a haphazard manner and without any involvement from the original design team.[1] All this will inevitably negatively impact the project's formal composition, its functional performance and even its structural integrity. These projects literally may, and often do, eventually fall apart.

What I am describing here is not a hypothetical scenario, but one that I have come across again and again. I am continuously confounded by how the extensive human and material resources dedicated to building projects are simply left to go to waste. It is one of many aspects of the intricate subject of sustainability that are very often unaddressed in the making of built projects in the developing world. As a result of this, I have come to see the value of the motto "if you can't maintain it, don't build it", and there are many projects I have come across that would have been better left un-built.[2]

The responsibility for ensuring the upkeep and maintenance of a built project falls almost completely on its owner, rather than the designer or builder. Even the best-designed and best-built projects need continuous maintenance and upkeep, and the field of facilities management, which is a well-established one in developed economies, is a response to this need. The field unfortunately does not even exist in many developing economies.

Still, it is interesting to note that so many projects everywhere are photographed for architectural publications very soon after they are completed and before they are subjected to any meaningful use. It is as if the architectural community views a project as being at its best at the moment of completion, and considers its trajectory from there to be only a downhill one. The Aga Khan Award for Architecture is unique in this context in that it acknowledges this challenge and therefore requires that projects nominated for the Award have been completed in the past six years and in use for one year. I would argue that even this period is not enough, and that a longer one is needed. In fact, an interesting exercise would be to revisit all the projects that have received the Award since its inception and until about 10 years ago (that is, the 2004 Award cycle) to see how they have fared. How a built project has fared over the years is definitely no less important than how it looked upon completion.

This brings me to the role of the architect, not only in a project's conception and implementation, but also in its post-occupancy phase. The architect's role, of course, has always been subservient to that of the building owner, who, after all, controls the monetary resources needed for constructing a project. This, of course, is not surprising. Even architects who have achieved a level of stardom still only have relatively limited decision-making authority in the design and construction of a project. This limited role diminishes, if not completely disappears (depending on context), after the project is completed.

More recently, the architect's role as the project's designer and form-maker, and even overall coordinator, seems to be seriously challenged as a result of the increased participation of a variety of new technical specialists connected to the making of built projects, which are becoming increasingly complex as design and construction projects. These include not only traditional specialists such as those involved in structures and HVAC (heating, ventilation and air conditioning), but also a wide range of newly emerging specialists in fields that address issues such as security, environmental sustainability, space utilisation, legal concerns and financial investment requirements. In this newly emerging setting, the architect is only one of a sizeable number of players with influence on the form-making process, and very well may be marginalised to become – at best – the project's "image maker".

And, of course, we should not forget that a significant part of our built environment is created without the participation of architects. This does not only apply to poorer economies, but also to advanced and affluent ones. In the United States, for example, there is no need to involve an architect in residential or other building types that do not exceed a specific size.[3] Here, the role of the architect is often taken over by the builder. In case an architect is engaged for such projects, it is most often simply because an owner wishes to make a statement about his/her elevated socio-economic status.

This exclusion of the architect from the making of built projects of course is even more prevalent in poorer economies. Here, let me provide an anecdotal example. I recently had an interesting conversation with an architect who had been studying the design and construction practices affecting residential buildings in a rural area in northern Jordan. She commented that the architect is almost always completely absent from these practices. The owner and contractor do not feel there is any need to involve an architect, and they believe that whatever an architect can do, they can do just as well. She added that the results of excluding the architect from the design process are disastrous. Admittedly, had people continued to build using the traditional materials and construction methods, as well as design and planning features that had been handed down from generation to generation and that had been fine-tuned over the years, one would have been able to easily make do without an architect. In such a case, many of the needed skill sets for these projects that the architect would have brought in already would have been mastered by the master builder. These traditional approaches towards building, however, have disappeared. A main reason for this is that they are no longer economical. It is far cheaper today to build using materials and components including cinder blocks, reinforced concrete, cement plastering, aluminium-frame windows… instead of load-bearing stone. This is the case even though many traditional building systems result in structures that last longer, have better thermal insulation capabilities, and are of a higher aesthetic value.

Since traditional construction approaches have been abandoned, and adequate widely spread comparable ones have yet to be developed, the state of building within the context of a place such as rural Jordan is characterised by utter confusion and incompetence. The plans for the residences do not work well at all. One ends up with rooms that are difficult to access or that do not receive any natural light or ventilation. One would also come across strange arrangements where a bathroom may only be accessed via the kitchen (as a poorly conceived way to save costs by limiting the length of the plumbing network), with only a curtain separating the two. Rooms unintentionally end up having different floor levels. An architect with very basic design capacities (not all architects admittedly may be described as such) should be able to ensure that such problems are avoided and that a residential plan would function with an acceptable level of practicality and efficiency. Most building owners and builders in such contexts, however, fully believe that the architect does not have any skills that they do not themselves have. If they believe that the architect has a skill that others do not possess, it would be to "make a building look more beautiful" and, for many, beauty is an unnecessary luxury they do not care about and feel they cannot afford. In the meantime, although significant resources are dedicated for making a building, these resources are used in a most inefficient and wasteful manner. Therefore, even though a house for many is their most valuable asset, this asset is dysfunctional on numerous levels.

The training of architects today, although in need of an overhaul, still provides them with diverse skills and considerable intellectual and technical versatility that can aid them in addressing the various challenges facing the built environment. Architects theoretically are still capable of playing a somewhat central role in the making – and also the managing – of built projects. There are two issues I can think of that have prevented architects from doing so in an effective manner. The first is that architects historically have cornered themselves into serving only clients with deep pockets, whether individuals or institutions, and thus have limited their potential clientele. On a certain level, this is somewhat understandable. The act of building is an expensive undertaking, and it is carried out by those who are able to dedicate considerable financial resources to it. I find this relation between architecture and wealth intriguing. For example, it is worth noting how a number of visionary architects who had attempted to develop high-quality, low-cost housing solutions ended up abandoning those attempts, and instead switched to designing projects for wealthy clients, whether individual or institutional. These include masters of modern architecture such as Mies van der Rohe and Le Corbusier, who dedicated considerable energies to developing inexpensive mass-produced housing prototypes during the 1920s, or Hassan Fathy, who worked on developing indigenous inexpensive architectural solutions for villagers in the Egyptian countryside during the 1940s. In contrast, it is worth noting that during the past two decades or so contemporary systems of industrial production have made so many consumer items, such as clothing, furniture and household items, electrical and electronic equipment, and even automobiles (the $2500 Tata car was a dominant news item not too long ago), available to a wide range of income groups at a scale not known in the past. In contrast, it seems as if the quality of housing available for most people continues to go down and its prices continue to go up.[4]

A second factor that I feel has prevented architects from being able to take a central role in the making of built projects is very much a self imposed one. Architects have restricted their role by faithfully subscribing to the romantic view of the architect as artist and form-maker. This is propagated in schools of architecture, where architects are conditioned to believe that professional success is most powerfully expressed when designing award-winning projects that are celebrated for their formal qualities. Interestingly enough, Hollywood has also contributed to propagating this romantic view of the architect to the public, sometimes giving it heroic dimensions, since the making of *The Fountainhead* in 1949.[5]

Form-making is definitely an integral part of what architects do. Architects, however, need to expand and even redefine their role so as to ensure a meaningful degree of relevance in today's ever-changing world. In order to achieve this, architects, for one thing, need to free themselves from working exclusively for wealthy clients, who view architects primarily as form-makers. They also need to redefine their role away from primarily creating or reshaping built form. Their role needs to be reconfigured to include managing built form and also innovatively resolving the challenges that inevitably emerge as buildings need to adapt to continuously changing and evolving uses brought about by demographic, social, economic and technological developments. Not every intervention that architects make in the built environment needs to involve creating new forms or reshaping existing ones, both of which are expensive and heavy-handed activities that involve destruction and construction.

A very inspiring example of such a rethinking of the role of the architect is presented by British architect Alastair Parvin, the co-founder of WikiHouse. In a recent TED talk, he presents new frontiers that architects may explore and that allow the profession to serve very wide segments of society rather than the fortunate few who have the financial means to hire architects.[6] Parvin points out the example of the school that approached an architectural office to completely reconfigure the interior of the school building because the corridors are too small for the number of students enrolled there. The corridors therefore could not handle the students who need to go through them at the beginning and end of the school day and during recesses. This led to all sorts of problems relating to congestion and bullying. The school understood that this project would cost a few million pounds. Architectural firms generally would welcome such a commission. This architectural office, however, came back to the school with the recommendation that they leave the building as it is and, instead, use staggered schedules for the students. They therefore came up with a solution that would cost a few hundred pounds (for installing new school bells) rather than a few million. Parvin adds that one would think that this office is driving itself out of business by making such recommendations. What it is doing, however, is to rethink the role of the architect in a manner that is not limited to the conventional role of constructing (and possibly tearing down) a structure, but that innovatively re-imagines how a structure may be used. This allows them to become relevant and valuable to a much wider segment of the population.

Parvin also presents WikiHouse (www.wikihouse.cc). Here, he has been involved in developing what he refers to as an open-source construction system for building a single-family house. WikiHouse is basically a big kit that is available online. Users can download a set of cutting files and physically produce pieces using computer-controlled cutting machines. They would then assemble these pieces together to create the skeleton of a house. Two to three people with no experience in construction can easily assemble the basic chassis of such a house. Parvin refers to this process as one that allows societies to move from a state of mass consumption to one of mass production, and that allows everybody to become actively involved in the making of the built environment. It also allows the architect to take on the role of social and economic enabler through designing such kits and making what architects do accessible to a wide segment of society.

The Award Juries have shortlisted and awarded a number of non-conventional building projects over the years. Examples have included the Sandbag Shelters in Ahwaz, Iran, by Nadir Khalili and the Post-Tsunami Housing project that Shigeru Ban Architects developed in Kirinda, Sri Lanka.[7] Both provide innovative solutions regarding how housing may be designed and constructed. Such solutions, however, remain few and far between. Additional solutions need to be developed. It seems we are still a long way from getting there.

What I have presented in this essay provides a very preliminary exploration of how architects may take part in redefining how built projects are designed and constructed, and how in doing so they may contribute to the process of democratising the process of making architecture while maintaining an important role in it. Such a goal remains in its infancy, but considerable advances can be made towards realising it. Architecture can and should be made more affordable and more participatory. Moreover, the skill sets that architects usually master can be made relevant to a much wider segment of the population rather than only to a privileged few. New technologies, new needs and new mindsets can bring about a revolution in how and by whom buildings are designed and made, and can completely reconfigure our conception of the built project.

1 For an engaging discussion of how buildings evolve with time, see Stewart Brand, *How Buildings Learn: What Happens After They're Built,* New York: Penguin Book, 1994.

2 Regarding the issue of post-occupancy maintenance in the developing world, see Mohammad al-Asad, "If You can't Maintain It, don't Build It", *The Jordan Times* (8 April 8, 2005). The article is also available online at http://csbe.org/e-publications-resources/urban-crossroads/if-you-can-t-maintain-it-don-t-build-it/ (accessed on 28 June 2013).

3 Regarding the projects that require the participation of an architect in the state of Nebraska in the United States, for example, see State of Nebraska Board of Engineers and Architects, "When do You Need an Architect or Professional Engineer in Nebraska?" The document is available online at www.ea.state.ne.us/when_do_you_need.html (accessed on 28 June 2013).

4 For a view on the relation between wealth and architecture, see Mohammad al-Asad, "Architecture for the Rich; Mere Shelter for the Poor", *The Jordan Times* (7 February 2008). The article is also available online at http://csbe.org/e-publications-resources/urban-crossroads/architecture-for-the-rich-mere-shelter-for-the-poor/ (accessed on 28 June 2013).

5 For an interesting take on how the film industry views architects, see Mindy Kaly, "Chick Flicks", *The New Yorker* (3 October 2011). The article is also available online at www.newyorker.com/humor/2011/10/03/111003sh_shouts_kaling?currentPage=2 (accessed on 28 June 2013).

6 Alastair Parvin's February 2013 TED Talk, "Architecture for the People by the People", is available online at www.ted.com/talks/alastair_parvin_architecture_for_the_people_by_the_people.html?%3Futm_medium=social&source=email&utm_source=email&utm_campaign=ios-share (accessed on 28 June 2013).

7 Information on the Sandbag Shelters and the Post-Tsunami Housing projects is available on the website of the Aga Khan Trust for Culture. See www.akdn.org/akaa_award9_awards_detail3.asp and www.akdn.org/architecture/project.asp?id=3519 (both accessed on 28 June 2013).

FROM PUBLIC SPACE TO PUBLIC SPHERE
Homi K. Bhabha

"It's our turn now
To puzzle the unborn. No world
Wears as well as it should, but mortal or not,
A world has still to be built."

W. H. Auden, *The Birth of Architecture*

My involvement with the Aga Khan Award for Architecture – as a member of both the Master Jury and the Steering Committee – has persuaded me that architecture is the midwife to "the good life." Many times a year His Highness the Aga Khan convenes us as a group – architects, artists, engineers, historians, planners, landscape designers, cultural critics – to conceive ways by which the afflictions of the global world might be alleviated by humane interventions and institutional innovations in the realm of the built environment. We are challenged, so to speak, "to puzzle the unborn", to think outside the box, to place ourselves ahead of the curve by engaging with problems, and seeking solutions that are emergent or incipient in the ongoing processes of social transformation. The potential for new infrastructural or planning initiatives; the viability of new building types; sustainability achieved through the deployment of local initiatives in the interest of new structural design or the invention of new materials; the creation of new communities of stakeholders through collaborations between the commercial sector, the state, microcredit banks and non-governmental organisations – these are only some of the ways in which "puzzling the unborn" produces *agents of change* – individual or institutional – capable of inaugurating new paradigms of social development and cultural progress.

While cultivating the seeds of invention as yet "unborn", the Award insists that we return with new resolve and fresh ideas to a world that has not worn as well as it should have. This is a world we know only too well: a world of inequality, unemployment, homelessness, illiteracy, disease, violence and ecological degradation. It is the resolute will of the Award to invest in the belief that "a world has *still* to be built" in the double meaning W. H. Auden gives to that phrase.

In one sense, *still* building the world is a continual, incremental activity – wherever we are in time and place, the world still remains to be built and rebuilt. We turn to the tasks of restoration and conservation to give new life to monuments and memorials, to revive built environments and natural resources that have suffered the wear and tear of nature's ferocity and the rapacity of human history. A second reading of the phrase – "mortal or not/a world has still to be built" – suggests that our spiritual and aesthetic desire for perfectibility joins with our ethical concerns for fairness and justice as we *aspire* towards ways of living and building that create new horizons for humanity. To believe that a world *still has to be built* in the aspirational sense is to introduce a cautionary note of "value" in the process of responding to pragmatic interests in concrete circumstances: how will *this* planning decision, or *this* choice of material, or *this* configuration of public space be seen by the populations of the future? In exercising our professional expertise how do we establish "best practices" that serve our contemporaries while creating enduring frameworks of value that will ensure the quality of life for those generations as yet "unborn"?

A wide repertoire of problems, ideas and aims circulates through the programmatic agenda of the Award because its concerns for the built environment are an integral part of its attempt to support and protect the establishment of civil society across the various geopolitical landscapes of the *umma* – some robust and stable, others volatile and vulnerable. His Highness has defined the core concept of civil society as made up of "institutions designed to advance the public good but powered by private energies". A vital connection between the Award and the other agencies of the Aga Khan Development Network (AKDN) is established through the contribution all these agencies make to strengthening the role of civil society across the *umma*.

A recent discussion of the AKDN Civil Society programme makes a cogent link between the "good society" and "public space": "Civil society can be seen as being drawn from three traditions: as part of society or associational life lived through groups and associations; as the kind of society that we want to see or the 'good society'; and as ideas about how society is formed and shaped in the domain of the public space where different views on issues – such as good governance – are expressed and negotiated."

Pluralism is the living link between the good society and public space, and architecture is the arc of this ancient and intimate connection. The ethics of the good society – democratic rights, equal opportunities, respect for the beliefs and customs of communities, the dignity of the individual – are protected and enacted in the governmental institutions that shape the public space – freedom of expression, dialogical democratic exchange, the provision of education, health, safety, work and other aspects of human security. Civil society combines the provision of social goods with the equitable representation of private and public bodies that work to protect and enhance the "quality of life". Professional associations, commercial enterprises, educational establishments, ethnic and religious associations, cultural institutions, organisations dedicated to advocacy for minority representation – these are all participants in the creation of civil society as it combines an ethical and political pluralism with the institutions of pluralist social systems. The AKDN is surely right when it suggests that civil society, at its best, works like an "ecosystem, an assemblage of different parts and connections that adds up to more than the sum of its parts".

Pluralism, as embraced by the Award, is a framework of ethical and cultural values articulated through the practice of architecture and the built environment. Its purpose is to spread tolerance, dialogue, collaboration and affiliation amongst diverse communities – national, migrant and diasporic – who are historically fated to live side by side in indigenous and foreign habitations. The pluralist perspective is committed to finding modes of communication and negotiation through which communities can play a decisive role – with the collaboration of architects, planners, designers and engineers – in deciding what they consider to be "the good life". Deliberating on such "quality of life" issues requires that the *local* conditions of living and building – customs, materials, work practices, traditions, hopes and dreams – have to play an important *normative* role in making any building decision. And such acts of deliberation, if they are going to embrace the plural interests of the whole community or society, require there to be a vibrant civil society that is capable of negotiating with the state on its own terms, while balancing the interests of specific groups.

Such a complex task is further complicated when the fast globalising *umma* is faced with the challenge of diversity both internally and externally. Multicultural societies are prone to the contestation of belief and custom, and only a confident civil society can turn these differences into a civil conversation between communities. Within ethnic and religious groups, who often find themselves marginalised in metropolitan societies, there is a sense of betrayal when second- and third-generation adherents seek other, less traditional affiliations. In parts of the *umma*, there is potential for conflict when particular ethnic or religious populations are divided between those who continue to live in the national home and those who live abroad but seek to have an indigenous influence. It would hardly be an exaggeration to say that the internal challenges and opportunities within civil society formations – where affiliations and solidarities have to be created from parts rather than wholes – are, on a smaller scale, true of the complex structure of the *umma as a whole* in our contemporary world.

To enhance the construction and cultivation of public space is, in the broadest terms, the mission of the Award. Its commitment to the promotion and protection of civil society allows the Award to engage with the problems of public space as part of a larger concern with the emergence of global "public spheres" – those democratic institutions and fora that ensure the freedom of the city; the intercultural expression of ideas, beliefs and customs; the open communication between individuals and communities; and the lively exchanges of commerce and technology. The concept of the public sphere has been too closely tied to Eurocentric ideas of the Enlightenment, whereas it has a wider relevance to the propagation of the ideals of civil society across the globe. Public space is the matrix of the public sphere: it provides the habitations of family life and social settlement; it creates public squares where the "people" congregate in recognition of their civic identities; it houses museums, schools and universities that turn legal and political citizens into cultural citizens; it provides channels of public transport that network the plural neighbourhoods of the *polis.* The public sphere convenes the built environment into a living organism that transforms the lives it supports, just as it is transformed by the inhabitants that render it alive.

A world has still to be built... Nothing must deter us from this truth. A worn-out world deserves our urgent attention. An unborn world deserves our creative intelligence. A world *has to be built* as best we know it, and as best we can do it, because that is our debt to the past and our duty to the future.

2013 AWARD STEERING COMMITTEE

His Highness the Aga Khan
Chairman

Mohammad al-Asad
Architect and architectural historian; Founder and Chairman, Center for the Study of the Built Environment, Amman, Jordan

Homi K. Bhabha
Cultural theoretician; Anne F. Rothenberg Professor of the Humanities in the Department of English and Director, Mahindra Humanities Center, Harvard University, Cambridge, USA

Norman Foster
Architect; Chairman, Foster + Partners, London, UK

Omar Abdulaziz Hallaj
Architect and development consultant, Damascus, Syria

Glenn Lowry
Art historian; Director, The Museum of Modern Art, New York City, USA

Rahul Mehrotra
Architect; Principal, RMA Architects, Mumbai, India, and Professor of Urban Design and Chair of the Department of Urban Planning and Design, Graduate School of Design, Harvard University, Cambridge, USA

Mohsen Mostafavi
Architect and educator; Dean and Alexander and Victoria Wiley Professor of Design, Graduate School of Design, Harvard University, Cambridge, USA

Farshid Moussavi
Architect; Principal, Farshid Moussavi Architecture, London and Professor in Practice of Architecture, Harvard University, Cambridge, USA

Han Tümertekin
Architect; Principal, Mimarlar Tasarim Danismanlik, Istanbul, Turkey

Farrokh Derakhshani
Director of the Award

2013 AWARD MASTER JURY

David Adjaye
Architect; Principal, Adjaye Associates, London, UK and Visiting Professor at Princeton University, New Jersey, USA

Howayda al-Harithy
Architect and architectural historian; Professor, Department of Architecture and Design, American University of Beirut, Lebanon

Michel Desvigne
Landscape architect; Founder, Agence Michel Desvigne, Paris, France

Mahmood Mamdani
Professor and Executive Director, Makerere Institute for Social Research (MISR), Makerere University, Kampala, Uganda, and Herbert Lehman Professor of Government, Columbia University, New York.

Kamil Merican
Architect; Principal Designer and CEO, Group Design Partnership, Kuala Lumpur, Malaysia

Toshiko Mori
Architect; Principal, Toshiko Mori Architect, New York City, USA, and Robert P. Hubbard Professor in the Practice of Architecture, Harvard University, Cambridge, USA

Shahzia Sikander
Artist, New York City, USA

Murat Tabanlıoğlu
Architect; Founder, Tabanlıoğlu Architects, Istanbul, Turkey

Wang Shu
Architect; Founder, Amateur Architecture Studio, and Head of the Architecture School, China Academy of Art, Hangzhou, China

2013 AWARD ON-SITE REVIEWERS

Sultan Barakat
Architect and academic; Professor of Politics, Founding Director of the Post-War Reconstruction and Development Unit (PRDU), University of York, UK

Ahmad Djuhara
Architect; Partner, Djuhara & Djuhara, Tangerang, Indonesia

Seif El Rashidi
Architectural historian; Coordinator, Durham World Heritage Site, UK

Shahira Fahmy
Architect; Principal, Shahira Fahmy Architects, Cairo, Egypt

Zainab Faruqui Ali
Architect; Professor of Architecture, University of Dammam, Saudi Arabia

Hanif Kara
Structural engineer; Design Director and Co-Founder, AKTII, London, UK, and Professor, Graduate School of Design, Harvard University, Cambridge, USA

Jateen Lad
Architect and environmental engineer; Principal, Aurospace, Pondicherry, India

Michele Lamprakos
Architectural historian and practitioner; Professor, School of Architecture, Planning, and Preservation, University of Maryland-College Park, USA

Laurence Loh
Conservation architect and cultural heritage expert; Managing Director, Arkitek LLA SDN BHD, Penang, Malaysia, and Associate Professor, University of Hong Kong

Abdul Wasay Najimi
Conservation architect and scholar; Senior Conservation Architect, Aga Khan Trust for Culture, and Visiting Professor at the architectural departments in Kabul University and Kabul Polytechnic University, Afghanistan

Hassan Radoine
Architect planner; Professor and Director, École Nationale d'Architecture, Rabat, Morocco

Wael Samhouri
Architect and urban designer; architect in private practice and Chair, Architecture Department, International University of Science and Technology, Damascus, Syria

Mamadou Jean-Charles Tall
Architect; Co-Director, J&T Architectes et Associés, and President of the Board, Collège universitaire d'architecture, Dakar, Senegal

RECIPIENTS OF THE AGA KHAN AWARD FOR ARCHITECTURE 1980–2013

2013
Salam Centre for Cardiac Surgery, Khartoum, Sudan
Rehabilitation of Tabriz Bazaar, Tabriz, Iran
Revitalisation of Birzeit Historic Centre, Birzeit, Palestine
Rabat-Salé Urban Infrastructure Project, Rabat and Salé, Morocco
Islamic Cemetery, Altach, Austria

2010
Wadi Hanifa Wetlands, Riyadh, Saudi Arabia
Revitalisation of the Hypercentre of Tunis, Tunisia
Madinat al-Zahra Museum, Cordoba, Spain
Ipekyol Textile Factory, Edirne, Turkey
Bridge School, Xiashi, Fujian Province, China

2007
Samir Kassir Square, Beirut, Lebanon
Rehabilitation of the City of Shibam, Wadi Hadhramaut, Yemen
Central Market, Koudougou, Burkina Faso
University of Technology Petronas, Bandar Seri Iskandar, Malaysia
Restoration of Amiriya Complex, Rada, Yemen
Moulmein Rise Residential Tower, Singapore
Royal Netherlands Embassy, Addis Ababa, Ethiopia
Rehabilitation of the Walled City of Nicosia, Cyprus
School in Rudrapur, Dinajpur, Bangladesh

2004
Bibliotheca Alexandrina, Alexandria, Egypt
Primary School, Gando, Burkina Faso
Sandbag Shelter Prototypes, various locations worldwide
Restoration of Al-Abbas Mosque, Asnaf, Yemen
Old City of Jerusalem Revitalisation Programme, Jerusalem
B2 House, Bükhüsun Village, Ayvacik, Turkey
Petronas Towers, Kuala Lumpur, Malaysia

2001
New Life for Old Structures, various locations, Iran
Aït Iktel, Abadou, Morocco
Kahere Eila Poultry Farming School, Koliagbe, Guinea
Nubian Museum, Aswan, Egypt
SOS Children's Village, Aqaba, Jordan
Olbia Social Centre, Antalya, Turkey
Bagh-e-Ferdowsi, Tehran, Iran
Datai Hotel, Pulau Langkawi, Malaysia

1998
Rehabilitation of Hebron Old Town, Hebron, Palestine
Slum Networking of Indore, Indore, India
Salinger Residence, Selangor, Malaysia
Lepers Hospital, Chopda Taluka, India
Tuwaiq Palace, Riyadh, Saudi Arabia
Alhamra Arts Council, Lahore, Pakistan
Vidhan Bhavan, Bhopal, India

1995
Restoration of Bukhara Old City, Bukhara, Uzbekistan
Conservation of Old Sana'a, Sana'a, Yemen
Hafsia Quarter II, Tunis, Tunisia
Khuda-ki-Basti Incremental Development Scheme, Hyderabad, Pakistan
Aranya Community Housing, Indore, India
Great Mosque and Redevelopment of the Old City Centre, Riyadh, Saudi Arabia
Menara Mesiniaga, Kuala Lumpur, Malaysia
Kaedi Regional Hospital, Kaedi, Mauritania
Mosque of the Grand National Assembly, Ankara, Turkey
Alliance Franco-Sénégalaise, Kaolack, Senegal
Re-Forestation Programme of the Middle East Technical University, Ankara, Turkey
Landscaping Integration of the Soekarno-Hatta Airport, Cengkareng, Indonesia

1992
Kairouan Conservation Programme, Kairouan, Tunisia
Palace Parks Programme, Istanbul, Turkey
Cultural Park for Children, Cairo, Egypt
East Wahdat Upgrading Programme, Amman, Jordan
Kampung Kali Cho-de, Yogyakarta, Indonesia
Stone Building System, Dar'a Province, Syria
Demir Holiday Village, Bodrum, Turkey
Panafrican Institute of Development, Ouagadougou, Burkina Faso
Entrepreneurship Development Institute of India, Ahmedabad, India

1989

Great Omari Mosque, Sidon, Lebanon
Rehabilitation of Asilah, Morocco
Grameen Bank Housing Programme, various locations, Bangladesh
Citra Niaga Urban Development, Samarinda, Indonesia
Gürel Family Summer Residence, Çanakkale, Turkey
Hayy Assafarat Landscaping, Riyadh, Saudi Arabia
Al-Kindi Plaza, Riyadh, Saudi Arabia
Sidi el-Aloui Primary School, Tunis, Tunisia
Corniche Mosque, Jeddah, Saudi Arabia
Ministry of Foreign Affairs, Riyadh, Saudi Arabia
National Assembly Building, Sher-e-Bangla Nagar, Dhaka, Bangladesh
Institut du Monde Arabe, Paris, France

1986

Social Security Complex, Istanbul, Turkey
Dar Lamane Housing, Casablanca, Morocco
Mostar Old Town, Mostar, Bosnia-Herzegovina
Al-Aqsa Mosque, al-Haram al-Sharif, Jerusalem
Yaama Mosque, Yaama, Tahoua, Niger
Bhong Mosque, Rahim-Yar Khan, Pakistan
Shushtar New Town, Shushtar, Iran
Kampung Kebalen Improvement, Surabaya, Indonesia
Ismaïlliya Development Projects, Ismaïliyya, Egypt
Saïd Naum Mosque, Jakarta, Indonesia
Historic Sites Development, Istanbul, Turkey

1983

Great Mosque of Niono, Niono, Mali
Sherefudin's White Mosque, Visoko, Bosnia-Herzegovina
Ramses Wissa Wassef Arts Centre, Giza, Egypt
Nail Çakirhan House, Akyaka Village, Turkey
Hafsia Quarter I, Tunis, Tunisia
Tanjong Jara Beach Hotel and Rantau Abang Visitors' Centre, Kuala Terranganu, Malaysia
Résidence Andalous, Sousse, Tunisia
Hajj Terminal, King Abdul Aziz International Airport, Jeddah, Saudi Arabia
Tomb of Shah Rukn-i-'Alam, Multan, Pakistan
Darb Qirmiz Quarter, Cairo, Egypt
Azem Palace, Damascus, Syria

1980

Kampung Improvement Programme, Jakarta, Indonesia
Pondok Pesantren Pabelan, Central Java, Indonesia
Ertegün House, Bodrum, Turkey
Turkish Historical Society, Ankara, Turkey
Mughal Sheraton Hotel, Agra, India
Conservation of Sidi Bou Saïd, Tunis, Tunisia
Rüstem Pasha Caravanserai, Edirne, Turkey
National Museum, Doha, Qatar
Ali Qapu, Chehel Sutun and Hasht Behesht, Isfahan, Iran
Halawa House, Agamy, Egypt
Medical Centre, Mopti, Mali
Water Towers, Kuwait City, Kuwait
Courtyard Houses, Agadir, Morocco
Inter-Continental Hotel and Conference Centre, Mecca, Saudi Arabia
Agricultural Training Centre, Nianing, Senegal

Photo Credits
Nazes Afroz: 292–293, 296–299; Agence pour l'Aménagement de la Vallée du Bouregreg: 187; Alhadi Albaridi: 240–247; Amir Anoushfar: 22–23, 138–145, 162–177; Iwan Baan: 74–79, 272–279; Emre Dörter: 327; Cemal Emden: 16–17, 24–25, 64–70, 90–93, 94-top, 95–96, 100–106, 126–133, 148–157, 190-top, 198–229, 250–257, 286-top, 287–289, 321, 325; Reha Günay: 326; He Shu: 260–263, 266–267; Anne de Henning: 20–21, 110–117, 118-top, 119-top, 121–123; Steven Hobbs: 264–265; Jateen Lad: 54–55, 57, 60–61; Maria Grazia Cutuli Foundation: 294; Salima Naji: 94-bottom; Neo Spot Organisation: 18–19, 180–189, 190-bottom, 191–194; Riwaq Photo Archive: 118-bottom, 119-bottom, 120; Dominic Sansoni: 285-bottom, 286-bottom; Kristian Skeie: 32–33, 344–345; Marwan Tahtah: 302–303, 306–311; UNRWA: 305; Vidour: 58, 59, 62; Eresh Weerasuriya: 282–283, 285-top, 289-bottom.

Drawings
All drawings are supplied by the architects.

Additional illustrations, videos and information about the 2013 projects and other background material is available at www.akdn.org/architecture

The activities of the 12th Cycle of the Aga Khan Award for Architecture (2011–13) have been completed in large part due to the contribution and support of the following people:

Aga Khan Trust for Culture
Luis Monreal, general manager
Sirwan Abdulaziz, accounting officer
Shiraz Allibhai, assistant manager
Audrey Giroud, archnet site administrator
Amanda Monney, executive assistant
Lobna Montasser, documentation
Van Nguyen, senior IT coordinator
William O'Reilly, collections manager
Sam Pickens, deputy director, AKDN communications
Ibai Rigby, project coordinator
Thê-Hông Tang-Lam, digital production officer
Marie-Martine de Techtermann, executive assistant

Award Secretariat
Farrokh Derakhshani, director
Nuha Ansari, project officer
Francesca Cantien, executive assistant
Nadia Siméon, documentation officer

Regional Coordinators
Fay Cheah, South-East Asia
Bahrom Yusupov, Central Asia

Research
Elchin Aliyev, Azerbaijan
Khaled Asfour, Egypt
Naima Chabbi-Chemrouk, Algeria
Anna Grichting, Qatar
Khadija Jamal-Shaban, Pakistan
Berend van der Lans, Africa
Yasser Mahgoub, Qatar
Thomas Stellmach, planning projects

Documentation Assistance
Khadija Buhadi
Maryam Fakhr-Brandt
Mandana Ghajar
Roland Graber
Harriet Graham
Abigail Grater
Rakhima Missidenti
Cyrus Samii

Photographers
Nazes Afroz
Alhadi Albaridi
Amir Anoushfar
Mehdi Benssid
Adrien Buchet
Cemal Emden
Anne de Henning
Laurent Saillant
Kristian Skeie
Marwan Tahtah
Mohanad Yaqubi

Film Crew
Ladan Anoushfar
Emma Brumpton
Ben Campbell
Stephen Hobbs
Maximilian Jacobson-Gonzalez
Talal Jawich
Gus Lamb
Romaine Lancaster
Mohanad Yaqubi
Melissa Walsh
Ivan Wood

Other contributors to the 2013 Award Cycle
Ipek Akpinar
Hana Alamuddin
Adham Al-Sayed
Waleed Al-Sayed
Abdelmoumen Benabdeljalil
Irma Boom
Eduard Bru
Müge Cengizkhan
Salma Samar Damluji
Banu Durmusoglu
Paul Finch
Maria Finders
Anvar Gasim-Zada
Elbay Gasim-Zadeh
Sandra Hiari
Lluis Hortet
Wang Hui
Sarah Ichioka
Justin Jaeckle
Omer Kanipak
Gökhan Karakus
Yu Kongjian
Laurence Liauw
Taraneh Meshkani
Larry Ng Lye Hock
Carla O'Donnell
Joe Osae Addo
Sandra Piesik
Olivia Poussot

Nasser O. Rabbat
Alice Rawsthorn
Paul Ress
Hossein Reza-Jorabi
Tuuli Saarela
Gözde Sevimli
Francis Sossah
Nader Tehrani
Fernando Varanda
Tanja Wranik
Farida Zabirova

As well as the 883 nominators and 432 architects who submitted projects.

ARCHITECTURE IS LIFE
AGA KHAN AWARD FOR ARCHITECTURE 2013

This monograph has been conceived by Mohsen Mostafavi and Farrokh Derakhshani on behalf of the Steering Committee of the 2013 Aga Khan Award for Architecture.

Project descriptions were assembled by Harriet Graham, based on reports prepared by the 2013 On-Site Project Reviewers.

Documentation materials have been compiled and reviewed by Shiraz Allibhai, William O'Reilly, Ibai Rigby and Nadia Siméon.

Copy-Editor: Harriet Graham

Design: Integral Lars Müller

Printing and Binding: Kösel, Altusried-Krugzell, Germany

Paper: 150 gsm, Lessebo Design Smooth White

Published by:
Lars Müller Publishers
Zurich, Switzerland
www.lars-mueller-publishers.com

©2013 The Aga Khan Award for Architecture
and Lars Müller Publishers, Zurich

No part of this book may be used or reproduced in any form or manner whatsoever without prior written permission, except in the case of brief quotations embodied in critical articles and reviews.

Aga Khan Award for Architecture
P.O. Box 2049
1211 Geneva 2
Switzerland
www.akdn.org/architecture

ISBN 978-3-03778-378-8

Printed in Germany

Portuguese version available by Dafne Editora
www.dafne.com.pt
ISBN 978-989-8217-26-4

Also available at Lars Müller Publishers:
Implicate & Explicate
Aga Khan Award for Architecture 2010
ISBN 978-3-03778-242-2